Praise for *How to Train a Happy Mind*

"This book is a clear well-lit path through the tangled thickets of psychological and spiritual ideas, tools, and advice—and it takes you directly to greater resilience, happiness, love, and inner peace. Honest and helpful, this book is a gem."

Rick Hanson, PhD, author of
Hardwiring Happiness, *Neurodharma*, and *Buddha's Brain*

"At last someone gives a simple and clear introduction, for regular spiritual seekers like any of us, to the most important of all meditations—beyond the healthy calm, the deeply transformative analysis to discover the reality of it all!"

Robert Thurman, PhD, author of
Inner Revolution and *Essential Tibetan Buddhism*

"Scott Snibbe has done a marvelous job of interpreting the timeless wisdom of Buddhist masters for a contemporary audience. *How to Train a Happy Mind* distills the essential points of classic lamrim (path to enlightenment) teachings in innovative and often humorous ways, including clear and practical instructions on how to begin meditating on these beneficial instructions."

Venerable Kathleen McDonald (Sangye Khadro),
author of *How to Meditate*

"The real test of a book is whether, when you have finished, you can put it to use in your life. Snibbe's book passes this test with flying colors—it is specifically designed to convey methods that can be put to use, and it does that with a really impressive clarity. I've found it helpful—I'm paying attention in new ways—maybe it's better to say I'm giving attention. It feels good. I suggest you give it a try!"

Kim Stanley Robinson, author of
The Ministry for the Future and *Red Mars*

For Venerable Lobsang Chokyi (1958–2014),
who first invited me to lead lamrim meditations,
then teased me for spending more time on love than suffering

HOW TO TRAIN A HAPPY MIND

A Skeptic's Path to Enlightenment

SCOTT SNIBBE

Foreword by
His Holiness the Dalai Lama

WATKINS
1893

How To Train a Happy Mind
Scott Snibbe

This edition first published in the UK and USA in 2024 by
Watkins, an imprint of Watkins Media Limited
Unit 11, Shepperton House
89-93 Shepperton Road
London
N1 3DF

enquiries@watkinspublishing.com

1 2 3 4 5 6 7 8 9 10

Designed and typeset by JCS Publishing Ltd.
Printed and bound in the United Kingdom by TJ Books Ltd.

A CIP record for this book is available from the British Library

ISBN: 978-1-78678-746-0 (Paperback)
ISBN: 978-1-78678-761-3 (eBook)

www.watkinspublishing.com

**The author has assigned all his proceeds from this book to the
nonprofit organization A Skeptic's Path to Enlightenment.**

CONTENTS

Foreword by His Holiness the Dalai Lama   vii

PART 1: ANALYTICAL MEDITATION AND THE MIND

1   Confessions of a Buddhist Skeptic   3
2   What Is Analytical Meditation?   15
3   How to Practice Analytical Meditation   31
4   What Is the Mind?   42

PART 2: STAGES OF THE PATH

5   Stage 1: The Precious Life   61
6   Stage 2: Embracing Impermanence   72
7   Stage 3: Mental Cause and Effect   83
8   Stage 4: What Do You Do When You Are Alone?   98
9   Stage 5: Am I More Important than Everyone
    Else in the Universe?   112
10 Stage 6: The Red Pill of Renunciation   135
11 Stage 7: What Is Love?   150
12 Stage 8, Part 1: How Things Exist   176
13 Stage 8, Part 2: Who Am I?   191
14 A Skeptic's Path to Enlightenment   208

Acknowledgments   224
Notes   226
Further Reading   235
About the Author   239

FOREWORD BY
HIS HOLINESS THE DALAI LAMA

In general, we can categorize Buddhism into three fields: science, philosophy, and religion. While Buddhist religion is the spiritual practice that concerns followers of the religion only, Buddhist science and philosophy have shown themselves of benefit to humanity at large, including even to non-believers.

Buddhist concepts of relying on reason and logic as well as mental development, including through our system of analytical meditation, have stood the test of scientific investigation. Increasingly scientists are beginning to recognize that there is benefit in combining the knowledge of Buddhist science with modern science. In my own way, I have been encouraging study and practice of these different aspects of Buddhism as I believe they can help make this world a better place. My own four commitments of promoting human values, religious harmony, Tibetan culture of nonviolence and compassion, and ancient Indian wisdom also have their basis in these different aspects of Buddhism.

I am therefore pleased to see this book, *How to Train a Happy Mind: A Skeptic's Path to Enlightenment*, by Scott Snibbe, that is geared towards informing the general reader about the fundamentals of Buddhism.

25 September 2023

PART I

ANALYTICAL MEDITATION AND THE MIND

I

CONFESSIONS OF A
BUDDHIST SKEPTIC

I am a Buddhist. But the purpose of this book isn't to make you a Buddhist. Geshe Tenzin Namdak once told me, "Buddhism is not meant to make more Buddhists, but to generate happy minds." That is the purpose of this book: to share a structured program of thought that brings happiness and meaning to your life, develops your best qualities, and deepens your connection to others, all without requiring religious belief.

How to Train a Happy Mind is based on a traditional sequence of meditations originally designed for Buddhist "professionals"—monks and nuns who have committed their lives to the ideal that the human mind can perfect its capacity for good to reach a state called enlightenment.

Over the past decade, with advice from my teachers and feedback from meditation students, I have distilled this thousand-year-old sequence into the eight stages contained in this book. They are presented in a form that is free from belief in anything beyond modern science's accepted view of reality and requires no specialized knowledge of Buddhism.

The meditations included with each stage come from the lesser-known tradition of *analytical meditation*, an active form of meditation that uses focused mental exercises to establish life-enhancing habits. With sufficient practice, these meditations empower you with the tools to let go of problems like anxiety, craving, and depression, and enhance natural virtues like resilience, compassion, and joy.

What is most powerful about this path is that its ways of seeing reality eventually become part of your everyday life, not only infusing it with meaning and purpose but also helping you to build better relationships—and even a better world.

The Buddha was a skeptic

Though I am now a Buddhist, some twenty-five years ago, I wasn't. I didn't believe in anything except what science and psychology teach us about the mysteries of our mind and the universe. Back then, I would have called myself a rational skeptic—someone who tries to stay curious and open, while remaining critical and logical. I felt skeptical about the supernatural beliefs of any religion, but open to the idea that there might be a systematic way to live a happy, meaningful life.

I was particularly open to any cures for the mental anguish of a twenty-something. At that time, my outward life appeared wonderful, but my inner life wasn't. When I woke up in the morning, I felt anxiety that seemed to come out of nowhere. When I encountered people, my spontaneous response to them—at least in my head—was often judgment. And throughout the day, I felt a recurring sense of dissatisfaction, even right after I had enjoyed something that was supposed to make me happy.

I can't explain why I broke up with my fiancée during that troubled time. I remember the reasons I told myself but, looking back, none of them made much sense. I simply felt dissatisfied. And instead of probing more deeply within myself to understand my dissatisfaction, I projected it on to the person closest to me.

Breaking up with my fiancée didn't eliminate my dissatisfaction, anxiety, or judgment. I changed my job, I changed where I lived, and I dated new people. But I still felt the same.

That's why, a few years later, I was open to my brother's invitation to a week of teachings with His Holiness the 14th Dalai Lama. For several years, my brother had been sending me books by the Dalai Lama, which, to be honest, I had difficulty deciphering. This time, instead of suggesting another book, my brother invited me to hear the world's best-known Buddhist speak in person.

I decided to go, not because I was a believer but because I was a skeptic. I was curious to learn if there really is an "art of happiness"—as the title of the Dalai Lama's bestselling book claims—and whether Buddhist philosophy and meditation offer such a path to happiness.

One of the first things the Dalai Lama said at the start of his five days of Buddhist teachings was, "Don't become a Buddhist." I had never heard a religious teacher tell a crowd not to follow his religion, so I was immediately disarmed by his message that Buddhism isn't a set of dogmas, rituals, and beliefs to blindly follow, but merely an invitation for us to try its mind-enhancing practices for ourselves.

The other provocative thing the Dalai Lama said during his lecture was that the Buddha told his followers to take none of his teachings on faith. Instead, the Buddha said that each of us must personally test his teachings through study, reflection, and meditation, just as he critically tested the ideas of his time. And if any of the Buddha's ideas prove to be invalid when we subject them to critical analysis, we should set them aside.

The Dalai Lama taught that the Buddha was a skeptic.

What is A Skeptic's Path to Enlightenment?

How to Train a Happy Mind presents an ordered series of meditations that I call A Skeptic's Path to Enlightenment. It is based on the same sequence the Dalai Lama taught the first time I saw him in person—the *lamrim*—a Tibetan term meaning "graduated path." Around a thousand years ago, the Indian Buddhist master Atisha Dipankara wrote the first lamrim text, *The Lamp for the Path to Enlightenment*. At the beginning of the fifteenth century, in his *Lamrim Chenmo*, the great Tibetan scholar Je Tsongkhapa refined the lamrim, setting it out in the form that inspires this book. Tsongkhapa's lamrim is a brilliant condensation of the Buddha's vast array of teachings into a systematic program that is said to lead its most devoted practitioners to a state of ultimate freedom.

The lamrim is a masterwork of metaphysics and moral philosophy that says nothing is random; everything, both material and mental, has a cause; and the mind works according to habit, so positive thoughts result in increments of happiness, while negative ones lead to increments of unhappiness. The lamrim says that life is immeasurably precious, everything is constantly changing, and the universe is a miraculous, interdependent continuum, of which we are an integral part. From practical mental habits to defensible universal laws, the lamrim gives us a path to transform our sadness, anger, and loneliness into happiness, compassion, and connection.

The lamrim was designed for monks and nuns in a Buddhist culture who were raised to believe past and future lives, karma, and literal hell and god realms as accepted truths. But even though it was written for fifteenth-century renunciates born into a Buddhist worldview, in more recent years it has also profoundly affected many skeptical non-monastics who, like me, have studied with Tibetan teachers exiled in the West.

As part of Tibetan Buddhism's second generation of Western students, I have studied the lamrim sequence for twenty years and meditate on each of its stages every morning. I won't pretend that I have mastered this path (as my wife can confirm), but I can say that when I'm able to recall the right lamrim topic to apply to a disturbing thought or situation, it invariably helps me respond with greater skill and kindness.

What is enlightenment?

As you work your way along the lamrim's graduated path, you train in a progressive sequence of meditations that develop virtues like kindness, compassion, and integrity. This path is said to culminate in *enlightenment*, the perfection of all your positive qualities and the elimination of all your negative ones. In this state, you shed the illusion of your ego, realize the interdependent nature of all phenomena, and achieve happiness and mental stability that no longer rely on your external circumstances. But is enlightenment an idea that skeptics can convince themselves is true?

During a 2007 talk in San Francisco, I heard someone ask the Dalai Lama about another ideal that helped me better understand how believing in enlightenment could be helpful. The questioner asked, "Isn't it naive to believe in the possibility of world peace?"

The Dalai Lama paused at this question. And then I remember him saying that, yes, realistically, there is always going to be some fighting on our planet. However, when you have the ideal of world peace as your goal, it means that you make the most progress toward attaining that ideal—more progress than someone who has a lesser goal, or none at all.

The Dalai Lama's practical optimism made me realize that, just as peace activists are motivated by their ideal to end all wars, the ideal of enlightenment can set you on a lifetime's journey to expand your best qualities, let go of destructive emotions, and become a force for good in the world—even if you have doubts that a complete and final enlightenment is possible.

In the course of my years practicing Buddhism, the skepticism I felt about many of its claims has gradually been satisfied through logic and meditative experience. But the concept of an ultimate enlightenment, beyond which you no longer evolve, is one that I continue to question. As I've shared my uncertainty with experts, one thing I have learned is that my understanding of a final enlightenment may be a misconception of what the Buddha taught.

When I interviewed Buddhist scholar Dr Jan Willis, she said that the term "enlightenment" doesn't really capture the flavor of the Sanskrit word for the Buddha's experience, which is better translated as "awakening":

"Enlightenment" is static. It's like a state. "He reached enlightenment." It feels final. Where's the fluidity in that? Whereas "awakening" is more a process. Most of my training has been in Tibetan Buddhism, but I go back to Zen stories often because that was my first encounter with Buddhism. I note that Zen talks about *satori* and *kensho*. I think this is correct because once satori is reached, then it's to be deepened. Once you have that insight, then you continue to work. It's not like, "Okay, I got it. I can leave the zendo now. Success was attained!" No. We have a glimpse of our buddha nature. We have a glimpse of our basic goodness. We have a glimpse of our minds, our true nature. And then we have to keep working.

The idea of enlightenment as awakening to our full potential feels more in line with the curious, open states of mind that my teachers encourage in meditation—where questions are more important than answers, and where each of us always has more to learn and further to grow.

A path for Buddhist experts adapted to skeptical beginners

In 2006, San Francisco's Tse Chen Ling Center for Tibetan Buddhist Studies invited me to start leading meditations. With an audience of beginners, I initially guided them according to the classic lamrim outlines. But as I did, I would sometimes cringe because, even in the earliest topics, the seemingly supernatural aspects of Buddhism are presented as givens.

For example, a common way to contemplate the preciousness of life in Buddhism is to explain that we've been forever propelled by invisible karmic forces through hell and god realms, reborn as a superhero, ghost, or turtle, until we finally earn a human form. In one sentence, the meditation asserts karma, rebirth, and other realms as accepted truths. I felt that teaching like this failed to meet the needs of non-Buddhist beginners to whom we had promised a practical introduction to meditation.

After experimentation, study, and discussions with my teachers, I became convinced that the lamrim's profound series of meditations could be adapted to guide modern skeptics who believe only in what science says about our minds and reality—what I believed in my twenties, and what most of my friends and colleagues still believe today.

But I doubt that I would have undertaken this project if the Dalai Lama himself hadn't been encouraging a scientific, secular approach to the Buddhist path for decades. In his 2011 book *Beyond Religion*, the Dalai Lama wrote that, "The time has come to find a way of thinking about spirituality and ethics that is beyond religion." And in more recent talks, His Holiness has specifically advised people to practice analytical meditation because of its power to steer us toward happy, meaningful lives in which we respect ourselves, our communities, and our planet.

Because of the Dalai Lama's books and talks, I felt that this project was aligned with his view—though I still questioned whether I was the right person to undertake it. The lamrim contains extraordinary gems of poetic insight into the human mind and the nature of reality, but it is also wrapped up in the cultural conventions of its time. Sifting out the timeless wisdom from elements that feel irrelevant to modern lives, unsupported by science, or at odds with contemporary values is a challenge to Buddhist practitioners of the twenty-first century—and one that I hope teachers more qualified than me will eventually resolve.

However, my teachers still encouraged me to take on this challenge—not because of any special realization on my part, but because they thought it would be useful for people to learn from someone with a life similar to theirs. Unlike a Buddhist monk or nun, I am someone with a partner, a child, and a job; a love of movies, music, and popular culture; and a mind filled with plenty of delusions.

In the Tibetan Buddhist tradition there is a list of extraordinary qualities that a teacher should have. These qualities are demonstrably beyond my level of practice so, even though I have led Buddhist talks and meditations for more than two decades, I still prefer to think of myself as a Buddhist "teaching assistant," someone you learn *with* rather than *from*. This type of person is sometimes called a "Dharma friend," where Dharma refers to those teachings that help us to develop our good qualities and understand reality.

In my role as a Buddhist teaching assistant, I've embraced the challenge of adapting the lamrim to a secular form in meditation classes, retreats, and the *Skeptic's Path to Enlightenment* podcast. Many topics, like meditating on compassion or the interdependent nature of reality, have required little modification from their classic outlines. Others, like the precious life and karma, have required substantial revision to make sense in the context of a modern scientific understanding of the universe.

At its core, the lamrim is a sequence that helps us to understand which thoughts promote a happy, satisfied life of meaning and connection, and which bring misery, longing, and loneliness. Though it has required some creative struggle to adapt this path to a modern form, I have tried to stay true to its practical essence, asking what are the mental habits that make us suffer, and what are the ones that make us happy?

How A Skeptic's Path to Enlightenment differs from Buddhism

Lama Yeshe, the founder of the Tibetan Buddhist centers where I learned the lamrim, had a vibrant, creative approach to the Dharma and was one of the first classically trained teachers to guide Western students. In 1983, near the end of his short life, he said, "Give up religion, give up Buddhism. Go beyond Buddhism. Put the essential aspect of the philosophy into scientific language." His entreaty further encouraged me to take on this project.

Rebellious writers are often given the advice, "Learn how to write a story before you change how stories are told." Similarly, it's useful to understand something of the particular flavor of Buddhism that the lamrim espouses before exploring its modification. *Buddhism* describes many different practices and traditions drawn from the diverse Asian cultures where it evolved. The flavor of Buddhism that inspires A Skeptic's Path to Enlightenment is called *Mahayana Buddhism*, in a form that thrived from the fifth to the twelfth centuries at India's Nalanda Monastery, the world's first residential university. This form of Buddhism later spread to Tibet, where it survived into modern times.

Maha means "great" and *yana* means "vehicle" but that doesn't mean Mahayana Buddhists think their Buddhism is the greatest. Mahayana Buddhism simply has the most expansive aspiration: to be of greatest benefit to all living beings. Driven by boundless compassion, the ideal of Mahayana Buddhists is to live the wholly altruistic life of a *bodhisattva*.

The Mahayana Buddhist tradition developed the rich and effective forms of analytical meditation shared in this book. Mahayana Buddhists also elaborated a uniquely subtle "middle way" view on the interdependent nature of reality that is surprisingly compatible with modern physics (discussed in chapters 12 and 13). When I use the word "Buddhism" in this book, I'm only referring to this Indo-Tibetan form of Mahayana Buddhism that I learned from my teachers, not Zen, Theravada, or other forms of Buddhism, which have slightly different takes on the Buddhist path.

Even though A Skeptic's Path to Enlightenment draws from authentic Mahayana Buddhist sources, it diverges from these teachings in significant ways. I focus on a psychological and science-based approach to cause and effect, rather than a belief in karmic seeds and their results. I focus on ways to make this one life meaningful, without requiring a belief in lives that come before and after. And I focus on the universe as we know it, made up of galaxies, stars, particles, and planets—especially this one planet we live on, where life emerged and evolved to become capable of understanding itself. Among the hundreds of sub-topics in the lamrim, I have singled out a few key meditations that have resonated most with skeptical students. And to maintain the flow of the book, I only discuss points of divergence from the Buddhist path when it is relevant for a non-Buddhist reader to better understand a topic.

My hope is that these meditations expand the benefit that the lamrim has offered millions of Buddhist practitioners over the centuries to include a modern, non-religious audience. I have tried to ground the path in scientifically accepted reality and scientists' current understanding of the mind. And even though I have received superb teachings and helpful advice from Buddhist masters in adapting this path, I am the only one to blame for any mistakes or lack of skill in its approach. I welcome feedback on how to improve this work in progress.

How to use this book

Following this first introductory chapter, chapters 2 and 3 explain what analytical meditation is and how to practice it. Chapter 4 offers a series of meditations to help understand the mind more deeply and how analytical meditation transforms it. Chapters 5 through 13 describe the eight analytical meditation stages that progressively develop your greatest potential: the precious life, impermanence, cause and effect, refuge, suffering, renunciation, compassion, and interdependence. Each chapter pairs a modern discussion of its topic with guided meditations. Memorizing or listening to a recording of the meditations can make them easier to practice than having to open your eyes to read the instructions. The book culminates in chapter 14, which presents the entire Skeptic's Path to Enlightenment sequence as a single meditation. Following that, there is a notes section, with the sources of key quotes and facts mentioned in each of the chapters, and a list of books for further reading.

You can skip around if you are excited to explore a particular stage or urgently need help in one area. However, the sequence of topics in *How to Train a Happy Mind* mirrors the Tibetan Buddhist lamrim. So, for the optimal experience, work through the chapters in order, as each stage prepares you for the next.

You can benefit from this book if you simply read it, taking away useful strategies to remember as you face life's challenges. However, it will be far more effective if you also meditate on the topics. To update a Buddhist metaphor for the twenty-first century, studying mind-training techniques without actually meditating is about as effective as watching an exercise video while sitting on the couch.

The lamrim says that there are three progressive levels to understanding its stages: hearing, reflecting, and meditating. It is only at the third level, when you meditate on a stage repeatedly, that you transcend your efforts made in analysis and start to respond spontaneously to life's difficulties in healthier ways.

An ideal way to experience this book is to read one chapter and then practice its meditations daily for a week. With the repetition that comes from regular meditation, you gradually move from thoughts and concepts to a deeply felt experience that transcends words. This type of heartfelt understanding is called a *realization*. One of my teachers explained the difference between thought and realization by comparing it to the difference between reading about love and falling in love.

Like falling in love, a realization is something you seem to feel in every cell of your body. It becomes "real" to you. Some Buddhist realizations are difficult to attain, like the lamrim's final step of realizing the ultimate nature of reality, because it requires us to analyze and transcend our sensory perceptions—and even our sense of self—that we've taken for granted our entire lives.

However, my teachers have said that most of the lamrim realizations aren't as difficult to achieve. If you practice a topic's meditation consistently for a few weeks, or with full focus during a meditation retreat, you can achieve its realization. Of course, realizations can also slip away. To remain with you, a realization needs to be refreshed regularly, which is why you keep meditating.

I've had genuine realizations myself, ones that have positively transformed my personality and encouraged me to keep trying with the more difficult topics. These have included moments when I realized with certainty that nothing lasts, yet felt courage instead of despair; moments when I felt an unshakeable happiness independent of pleasure and achievement; moments when the illusion of a lonely, self-centered me disappeared into a sense of blissful interdependence. Realizations like these aren't signs of enlightenment or being particularly special or highly evolved, they are simply the ordinary results of practicing an authentic path.

So, if you are a skeptic curious to probe life's biggest questions, yet unable to base your practice on unprovable beliefs, I invite you to explore your inner reality systematically through these eight stages of A Skeptic's Path to Enlightenment. Discover for yourself if you can experience meditation's higher purpose: to bring out your best qualities, deepen your connection to others, and lead a happy, meaningful life.

2

WHAT IS ANALYTICAL MEDITATION?

Over the past few years, meditation has become a popular therapy recommended to help people to sleep better, reduce stress, and aid concentration. Yet meditation is much more than a useful tool for treating distraction or restlessness. For Buddhists, meditation's deeper purpose is to strengthen the positive qualities we all naturally possess, like openness, compassion, kindness, generosity, patience, gratitude, and joy. The type of meditation that actively steers your mind toward these qualities is called *analytical meditation*.

Analytical meditation is a path to becoming a better human being. It helps you to develop a rich inner life, while actively enriching your outer life, too, deepening your connections to others and making you a force for a better world.

In the Tibetan Buddhist tradition, there are hundreds of different meditations that you can practice to develop specific positive qualities. But all these meditations boil down to two types: stabilizing meditation and analytical meditation.

Stabilizing meditation calms the mind

In *stabilizing meditation*, also popularly known as *mindfulness meditation*, you are totally honest and present with yourself, accepting whatever occurs in your body and mind without needing to act on it. Stabilizing meditation helps calm your mind and makes you less reactive. It is the form of meditation most people have already heard about, available widely in apps and courses. For some, it may be the only type of meditation they thought existed.

In stabilizing meditation, you slow down your thoughts and focus on some aspect of your body or mind. The most common object of focus for stabilizing meditation is the breath. Your breath is always with you and it is a reflection of your inner state. It's quick and shallow when you're nervous, slow and steady when you're calm. Meditating on the breath is an immediate way to connect your body with your mind, opening yourself up without judgment to whatever you are experiencing in the present moment.

Stabilizing meditation is an important part of every meditation session. Without mental stability, you can't focus on anything—whether it's work, a conversation, or meditation. That is why all the meditations in this book begin with a short stabilizing meditation on the breath to calm and focus your mind.

Analytical meditation changes the mind

The second, lesser-known type of meditation is analytical meditation. This form of meditation goes beyond watching your mind to actively steer it away from disturbing thoughts, like anxiety, fear, and craving; and toward beneficial ones, like satisfaction, joy, and generosity. Instead of calmly watching whatever comes into your mind like you do in stabilizing meditation, in analytical meditation you actively question what pops into your mind, and proactively cultivate beneficial thoughts and feelings that steer it toward openness, happiness, and compassion.

Analytical meditation acknowledges that every single thought you have programs your mind in one way or another. The recently discovered principle of neuroplasticity backs this up, demonstrating how your every thought reinforces neural structures in the brain, making that thought more likely to occur later. Watching a movie, reading a book, or scrolling social media all modify your brain so that you think or act differently in the future. Advertisements work on this principle, reinforcing the thought that there is something you lack which will make your life complete. Your interactions with media, colleagues, family, and friends all unconsciously shape your mind too.

Analytical meditation is a way to take conscious control over your mind's habits instead of letting them be unconsciously programmed by your interactions with the people and the world around you. This form of meditation works in a similar way to cognitive behavioral therapy, which uses logic to recognize distorted thoughts and then trains your mind toward healthier responses. It is also similar to positive psychology, which expands beyond merely treating mental problems and on to fostering a rich, thriving life. Through stories, critical thinking, and reason, analytical meditation steers your mind toward what Abraham Lincoln called "the better angels of our nature."

Something encouraging I've noticed when leading analytical meditation sessions is that many people—even beginners—can give their full attention to an analytical meditation, while they have far more trouble maintaining the single-pointed focus of a stabilizing meditation. I think this is because we are so used to watching TV and listening to stories. And, ultimately, analytical meditation is just another type of story—one we tell ourselves with our eyes closed, sitting on a cushion, that helps us to better understand our minds and reality.

Despite analytical meditation being easier to pick up than stabilizing meditation, it is still important to practice both types of meditation. Stabilizing meditation calms and focuses the mind, while analytical meditation changes the mind. That's why you include both in a meditation session. A session often begins with a stabilizing meditation to calm your mind, moves on to mentally active analytical meditation to transform it, then returns to a stabilizing meditation to deepen insights from the analytical meditation, transforming them into heartfelt realizations.

Why practice analytical meditation?

After I first heard the Dalai Lama explain analytical meditation, I began studying Tibetan Buddhism with Geshe Ngawang Dakpa in San Francisco, and committed to meditate daily. Soon, I experienced some of the initial therapeutic benefits of meditation, like reduced anxiety and more restful sleep.

But I also started noticing subtle changes in my personality: instead of feeling judgmental, I felt more present and open to the people around me; instead of feeling anxious, I felt more at ease; and instead of wanting to ignore or escape others' problems, I felt the compassionate wish to help in whatever way I could. I saw for myself that meditation isn't simply about feeling better: it's about transforming who you are in ways that strengthen your connection to others and awaken you to the changing, interdependent nature of reality.

The Buddhist explanation for such transformations begins by acknowledging that we are each plagued by thoughts and emotions that agitate our minds, like anger, addiction, jealousy, and self-centeredness. It then admits that emotions we might ordinarily think of as positive can be agitating, too, like craving a cup of coffee, longing for someone's touch, or raging at the world's injustice. While nourishment, intimacy, and social action are encouraged in Buddhism, the distressed, egocentric way that we sometimes approach these experiences can negate the benefit we would otherwise reap from positive acts.

I found the Tibetan Buddhist view on mind training particularly attractive—and you may, too—because it doesn't require you to give up pleasure, work, relationships, or even conflict. It simply gives you the contemplative tools to let go of the despair, addiction, fear, and rage that sometimes accompany them by admitting that most of our agitation comes from how we react to experiences and not the experiences themselves.

Have you ever longed for the next cookie, even as you were eating the first? Or "swiped right" in a dating app, looking for your next hook-up only moments after enjoying your last? A smoker I know once told me about reaching for a cigarette when he already had one lit in his hand. You can be gripped by cravings even as you strive to satisfy them.

But with an unagitated mind, as you experience pleasure, success, or human connection, you enjoy these moments more fully—far more than when you are gripped by compulsive desire. You are able to feel wholly present for pleasure without fearing it will vanish or grasping for its return.

Achieving such presence requires a combination of stabilizing and analytical meditation. Stabilizing meditation helps you to become aware of your thoughts without acting on them. Analytical meditation then gives you the tools to counter delusions like craving, anger, and apathy by consciously choosing new thoughts and actions to replace your sometimes unhelpful automatic ones.

There's a stereotype that the pinnacle of meditation is a peaceful yogi sitting on a mountaintop in a state of total acceptance of everything that happens, good or bad. But checking out of the world to give up on your hopes and dreams isn't how I was taught to approach this path. The state of contentedness that results from a sustained meditation practice means feeling an unshakeable sense of self-respect, purpose, and care for others—not indifferent detachment.

Analytical meditation helps you to stay engaged with the world while choosing activities that give your life the greatest meaning, purpose, and connection. Instead of feeling anxiety, frustration, and craving, you feel happy and present. You can pursue your goals while still maintaining the realistic view that external achievement brings only temporary satisfaction. Then, even if you fail to achieve your dreams, you still maintain your happiness and presence, with a stable sense that the real causes of happiness lie within your mind and not outside it.

Of course, there is nothing trivial about external sources of happiness, and everyone needs and deserves food, shelter, security, medical care, education, and loved ones. But in

Buddhism there is another dimension to happiness and well-being that comes from within, which we can achieve through a combination of outer behavior and inner contemplation.

On the outside, Buddhist ethics explain how a life oriented around non-violence and kindness gives you a sense of well-being that results from a clear conscience. On the inside, the Buddhist view is that your mind itself can be a wellspring of happiness that comes from cultivating compassion and gaining insight into the nature of reality—when you discover who you are at the deepest levels of your awareness.

To start out on this path of self-awareness, one of the simplest analytical meditations you can practice is to consider that you are not your thoughts. In this type of analytical meditation, there is no need to clear your mind of thoughts. You simply stop becoming wholly absorbed in them. You start to observe thoughts objectively, like a scientist in a laboratory, analyzing what they are and determining which bring happiness and which create agitation.

With practice, you can carry this technique into daily life. You can become aware of the anger arising at your boss, then consciously let it go. You can accept your anxiety in the face of a setback, then move past it to work on a solution. You can notice your compulsive desire for an attractive body, then let it dissolve into the ease and satisfaction of simply being alive.

A Swiss Army knife for the mind

This book's eight stages and their corresponding analytical meditations can be practiced in quiet contemplation or in everyday life. In a morning meditation, you might deliberately choose the stage that corresponds to the quality you want to cultivate that day. Or when facing a problem in your daily life, you can recall a stage's formula and apply it immediately to whatever agitation is arising in your mind. In this way, the sequence is like a Swiss Army knife for the mind: it offers you a collection of tools to address whatever mental challenge you face.

How exactly do these tools manage to transform your mind? The Buddhist view is that most mental problems arise from living out of sync with reality. Awakening your potential for happiness and benevolence comes about through meditating on more accurate ways to see yourself and the world around you.

As this process unfolds, "character" may be the closest word to describe what analytical meditation develops within you, with each stage promoting specific virtues. Table 1 shows the analytical meditation stages of A Skeptic's Path to Enlightenment, with examples of the real-world problems they address and the resulting benefits they bring to your character, ranging from generosity to wonder.

Analytical meditation is for healthy minds

When I received the instructions for analytical meditation, they came with the caveat that these practices are generally meant for healthy minds. Some scientific studies back up my teachers' warning: in a disturbed mental state, meditation can cause you to ruminate on your problems rather than let them go, or lead to dissociation or denial.

If you are suffering from a psychological illness or disorder, please consult a mental health professional before trying the meditations in this book. There are experts who focus on the careful application of clinically proven meditation techniques to treat mental illness and disorders like trauma and clinical depression. I am not such an expert and *How to Train a Happy Mind* isn't designed to treat diagnosed mental illness.

Meditating for the wrong reasons

Even with a healthy mind and authentic instructions, there are other ways that meditation can fail to realize its beneficial effects. One of the key ways in which this happens is when you

Table I: Analytical meditation stages of A Skeptic's Path to Enlightenment

Chapters	Stages	Real-world problems	Character benefits
5 Stage 1: The Precious Life	Precious life	Boredom, apathy, hopelessness, depression	Gratitude, responsibility, enthusiasm, awe
6 Stage 2: Embracing Impermanence	Impermanence	Loss, illness, break-ups, grief, injustice	Gratitude, humility, acceptance, hope, courage
7 Stage 3: Mental Cause and Effect	Cause and effect	Frustration, anger, resentment, self-criticism, judgment, guilt, despair	Ethical behavior, patience, empathy, self-acceptance, forgiveness, responsibility, determination
8 Stage 4: What Do You Do When You Are Alone?	Refuge	Addiction, craving, self-loathing, judgment, conflict	Self-respect, satisfaction, equanimity, admiration, courage
9 Stage 5: Am I More Important than Everyone Else in the Universe?	Suffering	Anger, craving, addiction, self-centeredness, unhealthy lifestyle	Responsibility, self-control, compassion, patience, healthy living
10 Stage 6: The Red Pill of Renunciation	Renunciation	Denial, addiction, anger, craving, competitiveness	Self-compassion, self-confidence, generosity, acceptance, courage, contentment
11 Stage 7: What Is Love?	Compassion	Loneliness, selfishness, neediness	Kindness, generosity, compassion, joy
12 Stage 8, Part 1: How Things Exist 13 Stage 8, Part 2: Who Am I?	Interdependence	Frustration, conflict, despair, loneliness, disconnection, selfishness	Openness, curiosity, wonder, responsibility, connectedness, selflessness

meditate with an unhealthy motivation. I've been meditating for over twenty years, but I can now see that I sometimes used the stabilizing effects of meditation more to achieve worldly goals than to bring out my best qualities. My meditation became an escape to a spiritual "happy place" that relaxed and restored me after a stressful day. But outside of meditation, I only ramped up my pace, piling on projects that weren't necessarily that great for me or for the world.

Using meditation to escape problems rather than confront them is sometimes called "spiritual bypass." Spiritual bypass is the pitfall of practicing mindfulness without the essential complements of ethics, compassion, and wisdom. As a result, instead of changing the way you think and act in the world for the better, your meditation becomes a technique merely to escape your troubles for a while, or, worse, to recharge before you go out and create more trouble.

The ways in which the military employs meditation provides a useful example. Veterans are taught mindfulness meditation to help them overcome post-traumatic stress disorder. But active soldiers are also trained in mindfulness techniques that enable them to remain laser-focused on killing another human being. This extreme example shows that meditation can not only be used to let go of disturbing thoughts and emotions but even to disregard our natural aversion to killing another human being.

When I think of the worldly or even harmful ways in which meditation can be used, I remember Darth Vader in *The Empire Strikes Back* (my favorite Star Wars film). If you've seen it, you may recall how the Dark Lord meditates all through that movie. In fact, it seems like whenever Vader isn't killing people, he's meditating. He retreats to a giant black egg that opens like an evil lotus to mindfully watch the deepest, most even breaths you've ever heard.

Don't be like Darth Vader. It is entirely possible to have a negative, selfish, or worldly motivation for meditating. I've done it myself when I've meditated to bypass the pain of doing work I didn't believe in instead of facing the difficult prospect of quitting my job; or when I meditated to momentarily feel better about a harmful habit that I had no intention of letting go.

A simple way to ensure that your meditation serves a beneficial purpose is to begin each meditation session with a good intention: determining to weaken your disturbing states of mind and to cultivate beneficial ones; resolving to bring joy to others' lives and to ease their pain; deciding to see the fleeting nature of life and make the most of it; committing to becoming fully alive and aware in the present moment. The intention you set for meditation is essential in the Buddhist tradition, so it is usually established right at the start of every session in a stage of your practice called *motivation*.

Meditation isn't only for when you feel bad

People often come to meditation at a low point in their life, when they're overwhelmed by setbacks, anxiety, fear, or craving. Wanting to be free from mental problems is a powerful force that can drive you to start a meditation practice. And my own experience confirms that meditation, with the right teacher and techniques, can ease these problems.

But one pitfall of coming to meditation at a time of desperation is that, once you get over your crisis, you might also abandon your practice. Yet that's like giving up a new exercise routine just as your body is starting to get healthy and strong. Meditation, like physical exercise, not only makes your mind healthy but also keeps it that way, helping it to grow more and more toward its highest potential for happiness, compassion, and wisdom.

There are also people who come to meditation when their life—at least on the surface—looks great. Having achieved their goals, they start to ask, "Is that all? Why don't I feel satisfied? Why am I still worrying? Why am I still competing, craving, and getting angry?" These were the questions plaguing me when I came to meditation—when I had attained the accessories of a happy life, yet still felt dissatisfied inside. Finally, I had the epiphany that my problems came more from within my mind than outside it. And it seemed likely that I would find a more lasting source of happiness within my own mind, too, rather than in worldly success, a comfortable life, or even a loving family and supportive friends.

This path of privilege was how the Buddha himself came to meditation. He lived an opulent, sheltered life as a prince, with every luxury of his time and a loving family. But when he eventually discovered the universal sufferings of sickness, aging, and death, he abandoned his billionaire lifestyle to become a homeless yogi. Through meditation, he eventually found an unshakeable inner happiness and a life of meaning and purpose that he declared accessible to any human being who makes the effort to achieve it.

Meditation isn't relaxing

Another instructive example from the Buddha's life is that he did not choose to meditate in the wilderness as a way to relax. The Buddha's luxurious life of the finest massages and masalas was probably a lot more relaxing than wandering ancient India begging for food and sleeping outdoors. And it is still true today that you may not find meditation the most relaxing activity. For most people, there are easier ways to relax than closing your eyes and sitting on a cushion to explore the depths of your psyche.

You can relax by going for a walk, listening to music, taking a bath, or enjoying a glass of wine. You can relax at a sports bar, streaming videos, shopping, or smoking a joint. People do all these things to relax and they can be relaxing. Trying to meditate, though, can sometimes feel difficult, frustrating, or like a chore you don't want to do.

So why choose meditation over a bubble bath? Because no other relaxing activity on its own enhances your best qualities, diminishes your disturbing states of mind, and helps you to better serve the world. *That* is the purpose of meditation: to bring out your best qualities and to benefit others. Meditation can be a powerful way to relax—one that requires no special equipment, substances, or setting. In fact, relaxation is critical to effective meditation. But if you are only coming to meditation to relax, it may compare unfavorably to binge-watching your favorite TV show.

Understanding the unique power of meditation to build character, meaning, and connection helps keep you on the cushion even when it is difficult. In fact, the times when meditation feels hard may well be your *best* sessions because you aren't meditating solely for pleasure but also for meditation's long-term beneficial effects on your character and your relationships. This is another way in which meditation is similar to physical exercise—neither is unfailingly pleasurable, but we do them because of the long-term benefits they have on our body and mind.

Meditation also isn't spacing out, another relaxing activity. The state of mind you cultivate during meditation is alert and focused. It's the same level of attention you have while engrossed in your favorite TV show. But how do you develop that kind of single-pointed focus for objects of meditation?

You may already know how to meditate

If you've tried the most common meditation of watching your breath, you have probably noticed how difficult it is to give it your full attention. Your mind drifts, thinking of plans, regrets, the pain in your knees, or what's for lunch. It can be discouraging to see how distracted you get trying to pay attention to something so seemingly simple.

Yet in daily life, we are able to focus on objects other than the breath. We can focus single-pointedly while working hard on something we believe in, or when we listen to music or play sports. When we desperately want something that matters to us, we can focus on it for hours without drifting away: fantasizing about winning someone's affections, finding a job, earning a windfall, or even yearning for peace or justice. When we're upset, we can also stay with those thoughts for long stretches without distraction, ruminating on loneliness, resentment, or anger.

This ability to focus on things we want or don't want shows that we already have the power to concentrate. Analytical meditation just redirects our natural power of attention toward beneficial states of mind.

Science is confirming the benefits of meditation

A skeptic might ask if analytical meditation really does bring out the mind's best qualities. One way I became convinced of this was by spending time with great Buddhist teachers who had practiced these forms of meditation for decades. Their stable minds and compassionate behavior offered me direct, powerful evidence that analytical meditation really does develop the positive qualities it claims to.

Still, you could argue that these meditation masters were just born that way, like gifted artists, musicians, or athletes. That's why, around the turn of the millennium, scientists began to study the effects of meditation systematically—in many cases spurred by scientific dialogues they had had with the Dalai Lama through his work with the Mind & Life Institute. Some twenty years later, there is mounting evidence that validates many of the claims made by Buddhist teachings about meditation.

The therapeutic effects of meditation on reducing stress and anxiety, and increasing focus are the aspects that have been studied most. But there is also growing evidence for the virtue-enhancing effects of meditation. Peer-reviewed scientific studies by scientists such as Richard Davidson of the Center for Healthy Minds have measured empirically how meditation improves health, happiness, self-control, productivity, and our social connections to others. Experiments like his validate the claim that happiness and well-being are skills that you can train yourself in through meditation, not innate abilities that are fixed at birth.

However, most of these studies have been conducted on mindfulness meditation. Virtually no scientific papers mention analytical meditation by name, though scientists have studied compassion meditation, which is one form of analytical meditation. Richard Davidson is also a pioneer in this area, and the results of his groundbreaking research demonstrate how compassion meditation does indeed increase activity in areas of the brain associated with empathy. Other studies have shown the ability of compassion meditation to not only increase empathy and compassion but also to reduce depression, anxiety, self-criticism, and shame.

The principle of neuroplasticity that Davidson has linked to meditation is one of the strongest scientific supports for the beneficial effects of meditation because it provides a mechanism for how each of our thoughts and actions changes our brain. We reinforce habits not only as children (as was long believed) but also into adulthood and old age. "Neurons that fire together, wire together," is how neuroscientists cheekily describe this capacity of the mind to train itself. Many books have been written on this subject, some of which I've listed in the notes and further reading sections at the back of this book. In particular, Dr Rick Hanson's lucid books *Buddha's Brain* and *Neurodharma* share many practical ways to shape our habits through meditation that are backed up by contemporary neuroscience.

Analytical meditation is a science of the mind

One point not to overlook is that, for centuries, analytical meditators have considered their own practice to be a mode of scientific inquiry. This is where the boundaries of science come up against inner subjective experience, posing the question of whether the mind looking at itself is a valid scientific instrument. For many good reasons, science has discounted subjective experience in favor of externally measurable criteria as its highest standard of proof. But even though neuroscientists and psychologists are now able to use fMRI scanners and other instruments to detect the biological correlates of mental states, technology still remains limited in its ability to probe our inner experiences.

Yet each of us still has a pressing need to steer our mind toward happiness, mental stability, and heartfelt connections with others. Analytical meditation offers an introspective form of the scientific method to discern for ourselves when we are genuinely happy and connected, and when we are only pretending to be; and which practices steer us toward positive states of mind and away from disturbing ones.

It's reasonable to be skeptical that our seemingly unreliable mind can measure and steer inner experience with the precision of a scientific study. But even here there is a parallel between science and analytical meditation, because Buddhists have not only refined analytical meditation empirically but also through public criticism and debate, over the course of many centuries. And being a skeptic today doesn't mean we should reject the claims made in Buddhism outright but that we should test and dispute them thoroughly—just like scientists.

Analytical meditation doesn't end when you get up off the cushion

Although I use the phrase "analytical meditation" throughout this book, the beneficial states of mind we cultivate in meditation aren't meant to end when we get up from the cushion. The point of meditation is to take those thoughts we nurture in a quiet place out into the world. Ultimately, our most important practice is in our daily lives: how we soothe one another's pain, share our joys, and improve the world.

This contradicts the common misconception that the goal of meditation is calm isolation. It's true that one measure of meditation's success is a more peaceful mind and a deep satisfaction in being alone. But my teacher, Venerable Kathleen McDonald, once shared with me Lama Yeshe's advice that the best measure of success in meditation is not how long you can concentrate, or how nice it feels when you are meditating, but whether your relationships improve. You measure the effectiveness of your meditation both through your own inner insights and the good you do in the world. To give a painfully revealing example, I can feel like I just had the most amazing meditation experience, then walk out and have an argument with my wife that makes me realize I still have a lot of work to do.

3

HOW TO PRACTICE ANALYTICAL MEDITATION

An effective meditation session—like a great movie, a delicious meal, or a perfect playlist—has an arc to it: a beginning, a middle, and an end. Sports are like this, too, as you start with gentle stretches, move into more challenging exertions, and then cool down. If you don't ease in and out of exercise in this way, you can injure yourself. I'm not saying you're going to hurt yourself if you skip meditation's preliminaries and conclusions. However, meditation can be a lot more effective when you condition your mind according to certain sequences.

Meditation posture

The first step of a meditation session is to arrange your body in a posture that supports alert inward focus. Sitting cross-legged on a cushion with a straight spine is a powerful way for the body to support mental clarity. But if your body doesn't allow this, sitting on a chair with your legs uncrossed and feet flat on the floor can be equally effective.

Placing your right hand over the left, palms-up with thumbs touching can also help to support stable concentration. The tension you feel between your thumbs acts like a little radio tuner that tells you when your focus is too tight or too loose. People often ask why you place the right hand atop the left in a meditation posture. Traditionally this is because the right hand, symbolizing enlightenment, covers the left hand, symbolizing delusions. When I first heard this, it felt like another swipe at left-handed people like myself, and reminded me of the sad day when, as a child, I learned that the Latin word for left is "sinister." So if you want to stand up for lefties and meditate with your left hand on top, I'm not going to stop you.

You can leave a little space between your arms and torso, which allows you to breathe deeply from your diaphragm and prevents your body from getting too hot. If you tilt your head down slightly and aim your gaze at the floor in front of you, it helps to remove tension in your neck and reduce distraction. Then you can let the muscles of your shoulders, brow, and face relax. A helpful technique to loosen your shoulders is to scrunch them up tight and then completely release them. There are contradictory instructions for what to do with your mouth in meditation, but the most common one I've found is to relax your jaw and touch your tongue to the roof of your mouth. This diminishes the need to swallow while meditating, which otherwise can pull you out of a deep focus.

Closing your eyes almost all the way can help to strengthen concentration by removing the distraction of your surroundings, while still allowing enough light in so you remain awake. You don't want to confuse sleep with meditation because, once you do, it can become a hard habit to break. If you find yourself getting sleepy while meditating, open your eyes wide, but try to let your gaze rest in space itself and not on any objects. However, if you become distracted with your eyes open, you can close them completely.

I include one last optional posture that isn't traditionally included in meditation instructions. If you like, gently turn up the corners of your mouth. Thich Nhat Hahn says, "Sometimes joy is the source of your smile, but sometimes your smile is the source of your joy." This is not only a Zen master's wisdom but has also been validated scientifically by measuring the neurochemical changes that occur when you smile. Smiling releases neuropeptides that reduce stress and increase the concentration of dopamine, serotonin, and endorphins, which in turn trigger good feelings, lower your heart rate and blood pressure, and can even relieve pain.

When you attend a meditation retreat, you get to see the wide variety of postures and props that best support each person's practice, which shows how everyone's body has different needs. The Buddha inclusively said, "Whether standing, walking, sitting, or lying down, as long as one is alert, one should be resolved on this mindfulness. This is called a sublime abiding here and now." His words seem to indicate that even kicking back on the couch might be an appropriate meditation posture, if you can maintain the alert mindfulness of the meditative mind.

Most of the time I do my meditation in a relaxed, cross-legged posture atop a cushion on the floor. But sometimes, when I'm tired or cold, when I'm traveling, or when I wake up in the middle of the night, I'll do my meditation propped up in bed, in an easy chair, in a park, or even in an airline seat. The routine of meditation is more important than your posture or location.

My teacher, Venerable René Feusi, also takes the Buddha's advice on more active ways to meditate, recording long meditations in his own voice that he listens to while out walking. This allows him to exercise and enjoy the natural world while he does his practice. Geshe Tashi Tsering told me that when he was the spiritual director of London's Jamyang Buddhist Centre, he liked to meditate while running along the city's streets because many analytical meditations—such as those on impermanence, compassion, and emptiness—gain power from observing real-life people and things. Meditating out in the world helps you remember that the whole point of analytical meditation is to incorporate its insights about reality into your everyday life.

Motivation

After arranging your body in a suitable posture, the next "warm-up" in meditation is to set your motivation. Without being self-critical, think about the mental qualities you would like to diminish, and those you want to cultivate. The motivation for meditation is one of the key steps that transforms meditation from something that is merely relaxing into something mind-enhancing.

Motivation also gives your meditation an ethical foundation. According to Buddhist ethics, this can be as simple as wishing to do your best to benefit others or, at the very least, not cause harm. Put into modern neuroscientific terms, setting a positive motivation at the beginning of a meditation session reinforces your brain's neurological pathways for meeting others with a good intention and doing good in the world.

Refuge

After setting your motivation, you can consider what you wish the results of your meditation to be—what Buddhists call *refuge*, which is the subject of chapter 8. One place to find refuge is in your own potential to live a meaningful, connected life, by being fully present to those around you and achieving a better understanding of your inner and outer realities. What would your life look like if you expanded your generosity, patience, and compassion? What would it be like to have a clearer sense of which actions lead to positive results, and a constant awareness of the impermanent, interdependent nature of reality?

When you contemplate these qualities and your potential to achieve them, it can be useful to give them a visual form, such as imaging a warm bright light suffused with these positive mental states that flows into you.

In a Buddhist tradition, refuge is rooted in the great teachers of its lineage, particularly the historical Buddha himself. But even in a non-religious form, it can be helpful to think about any people, living or historical, who manifest the qualities you aspire to. You can bring to mind kind people you know, like nurses, caregivers, and family members, or historical figures, like great leaders, human rights activists, or writers.

The biographies of the people you admire often reveal that they went on a journey from a more ordinary state of mind toward one of mental clarity and fulfillment, and a commitment to better the world. According to the Buddhist understanding of the mind, all of us have the same capacity to achieve these qualities. When you realize this, it helps you to see a path from an ordinary mind to one that is more open, compassionate, and wise.

Stabilizing meditation

A stabilizing meditation on the breath comes next—the practice that calms and focuses the mind. You can meditate on your breath for ten minutes, five minutes, or even just one. It's good to end this phase while you are still fresh and alert—to quit while you're ahead—so you build a positive relationship to practice. The last thing you want is to hate meditation, and it's easier to expand on an enjoyable habit, however small, than to set an unrealistic goal and abandon it after a few days.

Analytical meditation

After a stabilizing meditation, you move on to an analytical meditation—the active form of meditation that supports you in diminishing delusions and cultivating virtuous states of mind. Topics for analytical meditation range from love, compassion, and patience to the depth of the world's suffering, and even the mysteries of what happens during sleep, sexual ecstasy, and death.

While following the basic outline of an analytical meditation, you can elaborate on each topic using your own creativity and imagination. This is similar to how a jazz musician bases her performance on a song's melody and rhythm, but then colors it with her unique personality and style. Once you've learned the basic outlines, in many ways, analytical meditation is a process of improvisation.

Dedication

The last part of a meditation session is the *dedication*. This can be a reiteration of your motivation, in which you appreciate having gently acknowledged, accepted, and let go of disturbing states of mind, and recognized and cultivated beneficial ones. There is likely nothing better you could have done with your time, so you can feel wholehearted satisfaction at having even incrementally expanded your capacity for good.

The dedication at the end of a meditation session isn't just a feel-good party with yourself, though. It helps you carry the benefits of your meditation beyond the cushion. Like relaxation and entertainment, meditation can become a compartmentalized form of pleasant escapism. To avoid this and make its benefits flow into your everyday life, you aspire that your meditation will cause you to think, speak, and act in the most beneficial, connecting ways possible. The power of the dedication isn't mystical or magical. It is backed up by the principle of neuroplasticity. Thinking aspirational thoughts deepens their associated neural pathways, and thus increases the likelihood of those thoughts occurring again.

Establishing a daily meditation practice

Neuroplasticity also helps us understand how we form new habits, including a daily meditation practice. Neurologically, it's supposed to take about two months to establish a new habit. During this time, you need to make a conscious effort to meditate. Being modest yet consistent in your choice of the place, time, and duration of your meditation can help you to build up a routine. Later, once you have been meditating for a while, sitting down to meditate will become automatic, just like eating breakfast, brushing your teeth, or taking a shower.

Where to meditate

If possible, it's helpful to set aside a specific space in your home to meditate. You may be lucky enough to have a room that you can clear and dedicate to meditation. Otherwise, free up a corner of your bedroom or anywhere else you can sit uninterrupted for a while. Your bed can be a comfy place to meditate right after you've woken up or before you go to sleep. But if you meditate in bed, your focus is usually better if you sit up in a meditation posture on a pillow, like you would sit atop a cushion on the floor.

Buddhists set up an altar where they meditate, with a statue or picture of the Buddha. For a non-Buddhist, the ideal that a Buddha represents, of perfecting your best qualities, can be generalized instead to images of people and places you find inspiring. These could be as simple as a photograph of your favorite camping spot or a distant galaxy; pictures of teachers, leaders, humanitarians, activists, authors, artists, or your grandma. On traditional altars, candles, incense, and flowers are placed as offerings to the beings and qualities you respect, making tangible your commitment to the ideal of a controlled, compassionate mind. But if it motivates your practice, an altar like the one I had as a teenager—with cassette tapes of my favorite bands, origami creatures, a photo of Franz Kafka, and a miniature disco ball—might work just as well. The point is for it to inspire you, and the benefit is only to your mind.

When to meditate

For many people, the best time to meditate is in the morning, shortly after waking up. Your mind is often clearest then and your ability to focus at its greatest. If you live with others, another advantage is that you can rise before anyone else and enjoy some silent time alone. You can go to the bathroom, splash some water on your face, then sit down at your meditation place undisturbed.

If the morning doesn't work for you, you can, of course, choose other times. The challenge with meditating any time after you first wake up, though, is that it is easy for other things to get in the way of meditation, or for you to simply forget and break the continuity of your routine.

How long to meditate

When I asked my first teacher, Geshe Dakpa, how long I should meditate, he told me to start with five minutes a day. He gave me a short analytical meditation outline, like the one that follows at the end of this chapter, which I practiced for about a year. Then he told me to increase my practice to fifteen minutes, which I was also able to sustain for some time. Then, year after year, I continued to increase it further. It's not that a longer meditation session is always better—it's best to end your session before you get tired, or, worse, irritated by the meditation. But if it feels healthy for you, longer meditation sessions generally deepen the effects of your practice.

Over time, my meditation habit has become so routine that it is now more painful *not* to meditate each morning, because the benefits are so clear in setting the foundation for a happy, purposeful day. If I'm running short on time, I'd rather skip a little sleep, my shower, or even breakfast—but not meditation. Sometimes I abbreviate my practice, but I never skip it entirely.

A TEN-MINUTE MEDITATION

Each chapter in this book includes a short guided meditation. For this chapter, introducing the meditation session, I share a simple ten-minute practice that is a variation on a typical mindfulness meditation. Even if you have never tried meditation, you will find it easy to learn. The meditation becomes "analytical" when it moves from mindfully watching your thoughts to actively analyzing them as they pass through your mind.

This meditation is short enough to come back to as an initial daily practice that you can do in the morning when you wake up, in the evening before bed, or when you have a break during the day.

This first practice also introduces all the stages of a meditation session: posture, motivation, refuge, stabilizing meditation, analytical meditation, and a dedication to carry the meditative experience into your daily life. Each stage plays a part in building a meditation practice that goes beyond relaxation, steering your mind toward its greatest potential.

In the chapters that follow, I only describe the analytical meditation, along with any specific motivation or dedication. But before each of the meditations in this book, please add the preliminary stages described here— posture, motivation, refuge, and stabilizing on the breath— then make a short dedication afterward to complete your session.

Another reason I start out with this analytical variation on mindfulness is so you can compare it to some of the deeper ways of meditating on the mind that we explore in chapter 4.

POSTURE

Sit cross-legged on the floor, seated on a cushion, or on
a chair, with your legs uncrossed, feet flat on the floor.
Straighten your spine and place your hands palms up in
your lap—resting one on the other, with your thumbs
touching. Relax all the muscles in your back, shoulders, face,
and arms. Aim your gaze downward, a short distance in
front of you, and half-close your eyes.

MOTIVATION

Determine to go inward for a few minutes, to bring out
your natural good qualities, and let disturbing thoughts and
emotions, which aren't your deeper nature, gradually lessen
and disappear. You do this for your own happiness, which
you naturally deserve, and for the happiness and well-being
of the people and the world around you.

REFUGE

Think of all the best qualities a human can aspire to:
compassion, generosity, patience, enthusiasm. If you like,
think of people you know or know of who demonstrate
these qualities. Realize that virtue can be strengthened
over time with methods like the ones you are practicing
now. Just like highly realized people, you too have the
capacity to increase your kindness, generosity, patience,
and love, and decrease anger, craving, despair, and
indifference.

If you like, you can visualize these qualities as a space of
light in front of you. Then let this space come forward and
wash over you, melting through the boundaries of your
body so that it merges with your own mind.

STABILIZING ON THE BREATH

For a few minutes, bring your attention to your breath: at your nostrils as air comes in and out of your body, or at your abdomen as it rises and falls. As thoughts, memories, plans, sounds, sensations, or discomforts arise, let them disappear on their own—without engaging them and without pushing them away. Thoughts naturally fade away, and your attention returns to your breath.

ANALYTICAL MEDITATION: WATCHING THOUGHTS

Now, relax and allow anything at all to arise in your mind. Watch your thoughts from a distance without letting them consume you. You are not your thoughts.

Next, try to gently analyze your mental experiences. Still letting thoughts naturally arise and pass by, start to label your thoughts as you experience them: memory, plan, craving, love. Notice which ones make your mind feel more at ease and which ones agitate it.

DEDICATION

By becoming aware of your thoughts and feelings in meditation, may you be more present, open, and connected to yourself and to others today. May your good qualities of kindness, patience, and open-heartedness come out naturally. And may you more easily let go of disturbing thoughts and emotions, for the benefit of yourself and everyone you encounter.

4

WHAT IS THE MIND?

Two early attempts I made at meditation stand out in my memory. One was comically unsuccessful, the other profound. The first happened in my twenties, before I became a Buddhist. I was reading a book by Vietnamese Zen master Thich Nhat Hanh that made me curious enough to try meditating for the first time. I put down the book, sat up on my bed, and closed my eyes. Aside from the thoughts inside my head getting a bit louder and more annoying, nothing much happened, and I soon climbed off my bed and went about the rest of my day, wondering what I was missing.

The second experience was years later, during my first meditation retreat with Venerable René Feusi, who soon became my closest teacher. On the opening day of the retreat, my results weren't so different from that first time meditating on my bed. But during the next afternoon's session, guided by Venerable René's instructions, suddenly it was as though a door opened up on to another dimension, where I found myself at rest in a vast luminous space of awareness. I felt overwhelming peace and joy, and an expansive sense of being that I didn't want to leave. When I finally opened my eyes, I was surprised to find the meditation hall empty, with no idea how much time had passed.

It turns out that these two meditation experiences are examples of two distinct ways that Buddhists probe the mind. The first is examining the contents of the mind, our *mental factors*: the thoughts and feelings that arise there. The second is experiencing the mind itself, or *consciousness*, the state of awareness in which thoughts and feelings appear.

Both kinds of meditation are important, and I think the main reason my first amateur meditation session was unsuccessful is that I had no framework to better understand my mind. I experienced my thoughts naively, identifying with them and ruminating on them the way we do in everyday life.

Directly experiencing the mind

A core Buddhist view is that a lasting source of happiness can be found within your mind. But if that is really the case, then it's helpful to first understand Buddhism's definition of the mind and the mental factors that pass through it.

Buddhist models of the mind can differ from scientific models. That is because, in Buddhism, mental models are evaluated not only for their accuracy but also for how much they help us to develop a happier mind, closer relationships, and more compassionate communities.

In meditation—and in everyday life—I have found the Buddhist models of the mind not only helpful on a practical level but also awe-inspiring. And in this chapter, I try to give you a taste of these experiences.

First, I explain the mental factors that Buddhism describes as ever-present parts of the mind. Learning what these are has helped me to stop many harmful thoughts in their tracks and gain greater control over my own conflicts and addictions.

Then I explain lesser-known techniques for experiencing your consciousness directly. Analytical meditation doesn't simply try to convince you of the logic that "you are not your thoughts." It demonstrates this through direct experiences, like that first taste of consciousness I had with my teacher two decades ago. I have found that once meditators gain a glimpse of the subtle—and beautiful—aspects of their mind waiting for them just below its surface, it becomes easier to view themselves expansively, as far more than the sum of their cravings and aversions.

Traditionally, these *nature of mind* meditations are considered more advanced practices, but some of my teachers have shared them early on with students for the door-opening effect they can have on your mind. That is why I share them here too.

Five mental factors

According to Mahayana Buddhism, a cascade of five mental factors accompanies every moment of consciousness. Initially, I didn't find these factors all that relevant to transforming my mind—until someone taught me how to use them in everyday life.

First, your senses make *contact* with some visual, sonic, or tactile sensation. Through *perception*, your mind wraps these into bundles that it categorizes and names. Your mind also has a *feeling*—that a perception is pleasant, unpleasant, or neutral. And your mind moves its *attention* toward some perceptions and away from others. Based on your feeling about what you have perceived—whether that be a person, object, or idea— you have an *urge* to do something about it.

At first you may say, "Who cares? Contact, perception, feeling, attention, urge—why do I need to know this list?" The reason is that this sequence helps you to understand how your feelings are biased by past conditioning, how they are often exaggerated, how they lead to words and actions you might regret later—and how you can stop them in their tracks.

My lazy shortcut to making practical use of these five ever-present mental factors is to share the one place where it is said that you can stop the otherwise automatic cascade from contact to urge, which is at feeling. This is where mindfulness intersects so well with analytical meditation because, if you can slow your mind down right as you are experiencing pleasant, unpleasant, or neutral feelings, then you can consciously choose how to respond to those feelings instead of automatically following the urges they provoke.

Perception is psychological

Bias and exaggeration aren't only at work with our feelings and urges. Even at the earlier mental factor of perception, the Buddhist model of the mind explains how none of us has direct access to physical reality itself. Instead, what each of us apprehends are the mind's interpretation of processed sensory signals. From these, we then construct a model of reality.

Light is just the vibration of "invisible" electromagnetic energy at different frequencies. When those vibrations beam through your eyes to stimulate your brain, you mentally construct the illusion of distinct colors. No red, orange, yellow, green, or blue exist outside your mind. It is the same with sound: inherently "silent" variations in air pressure are transformed by your ears and brain into the mental constructs of noises, words, and music.

The reality we each fabricate is a "controlled hallucination," as neuroscientist Anil Seth describes it. The brain synthesizes a virtual inner reality by combining its prior expectations of reality with these incoming sensory signals.

Because perception is psychological, our imagination, memory, and dreams can feel just as real as the reality that perception constructs from our five senses. That is why Buddhism describes a sixth sense. This isn't an ability to see ghosts or predict the future; it is the mind's interior ability to produce images, sounds, and thoughts without sensory input.

In the Buddhist model of perception, then, our mind has the ability to differentiate objects from one another—bundling the constant stream of sensory and imaginative stimulation into discrete packages that we label as objects or concepts.

It can be disconcerting when you start to think about perceptions as mere collections of sensory signals because you start to realize that there really are no "objects" out there in the world. Objects are just convenient labels that we place on collections of sensory stimulation, imagination, and memory. That collection of energy and particles is me and that other collection is you. That is delicious chocolate and that is bitter medicine. That is the sweet voice of my partner and that is the annoying speech of the person I didn't vote for.

When we realize that perception lacks objective truth, it offers us yet another way to question the strong feelings and urges we experience in relation to the objects we perceive. It also gives us the opportunity to choose more beneficial ways of responding to them.

Feeling and emotion

The mental factor of feeling is our immediate reaction of *pleasant, unpleasant,* or *neutral* to the objects we perceive, whether real or imagined. Pleasant feelings make us want to repeat the experiences that provoked them, while unpleasant feelings make us want to avoid whatever brought them about. Neutral feelings evoke indifference.

The mental factor of feeling doesn't equate with emotions as we commonly understand them. In fact, the Buddhist psychological system has no analog for the Western term "emotion." Instead, emotions, from a Buddhist perspective, are combinations of the more primal mental factor of feeling and the thoughts that elaborate it.

Urge and karma

The mental factor of urge is more commonly called *intention* or *volition.* It is the part of your mind that drives you to do things—or at least to want to do things—in response to feeling. Urge gets you up off the couch.

In Buddhism, urge is also the dominant factor in the creation of *karma,* which is the imprints of actions from prior lives that affect experiences in this life. However, you can understand urge in a more practical way, without recourse to karma, because, whatever the mechanism, both Buddhists and scientists agree that our current thoughts and actions strengthen or weaken our future mental habits.

The mental factor of urge is elaborated into dozens of different states of mind that drive us to action. They can manifest as a resolve, a wish, or a grudge, but are always things that move us toward a mental or physical act, whether we follow through with it or not.

Once urge has been activated, it can be hard to stop its nearly automatic follow-through. But when we slow down the preceding mental factor of feeling, we can then pause urges even as strong as addiction, violence, or depression— in addition to their milder variations.

The fundamental goodness of the mind

When you probe your mind in analytical meditation, you often pay attention to whether the mental factors that arise within it are harmful or beneficial, and whether you want to let go of certain thoughts and encourage others.

Harmful states of mind are referred to as *delusions*—mental states that disturb you, like rage and addiction. Beneficial states of mind are the ones that make you feel satisfaction, self-respect, and presence. These may be gentle ones like compassion and kindness, or forceful ones like effort and awe.

When meditating, it can feel like your disturbing and beneficial thoughts are equal opponents, fighting one another like the little angels and devils that sometimes appear on people's shoulders in cartoons. But one of the most powerful claims of Buddhism is that our inner angels and devils aren't equal at all.

Despite how much you may have heard about its focus on suffering, Buddhists hold the optimistic view that the mind is fundamentally good. Beneficial states of mind are said to be our deepest ones, while disturbing states of mind, even though they sometimes overpower us, are superficial. We don't need to fight or demonize our delusions; we merely need to let them pass by without acting on them, and cultivate our more intrinsic states of goodness.

This claim of humanity's fundamental goodness is what Buddhists call our *buddha nature*. Scientists like Dacher Keltner and Robert Sapolsky have probed this idea in their research and found scientific support for it. Some evidence comes from studies that show how people's first instincts in a social situation are biased toward cooperation rather than selfishness. Other evidence comes from analyzing our bad behavior and finding that most of it stems from problems we exaggerate or imagine.

Of course, this research on human nature isn't definitive, and even Buddhists can be skeptical about the seemingly idyllic belief in our fundamental good nature. That's why some schools of Buddhism limit their optimism to the more defensible claim that the mind is simply changeable—and that it can change for the better.

MEDITATION ON MENTAL FACTORS

Mental factors are said to arise more or less automatically, conditioned by our habits and experiences, upbringing, culture, genetics, and anything else that strengthens or weakens the brain's neural pathways and the mind's tendencies.

Meditating on the mental factors of perception, feeling, and urge helps us to understand how uncolored perception turns into pleasant and unpleasant reactions. By slowing down this process and wholly accepting our feelings, we gain control over whether to release or act out the urges they normally provoke.

PRELIMINARIES

Begin by settling into your meditation posture. Set your motivation to gradually bring out the qualities of your mind that lead to happiness, connection, and positive action in the world. Then move on to practicing refuge and a stabilizing meditation on the breath.

PERCEPTION

Now bring your attention to the mental factor of perception. Let whatever sensory experiences naturally occur arise in your mind. Notice how your mind perceives voices in the distance, furniture in the room, tension in your muscles, air across your skin. Notice, too, how you attach a mental label to these bundles of sensory information so that each perception seems separate and clearly identified as a sound, sensation, or object.

Then notice how your continuous experience of thought also gets broken into discrete bundles: that's a memory, that's a plan, that's a worry. For a minute, look at thought through this lens of perception.

FEELING

Without trying to control what arises in your mind, now look at the mental factor of feeling. Let anything come naturally into your mind, paying attention only to the feeling associated with each perception. Whether a sound, a body sensation, a thought, or a memory, notice whether a pleasant, unpleasant, or neutral feeling accompanies it. Completely accept your feelings without overly identifying with them.

URGE

Now notice the component of your mind that wants to do something about your feelings. This might be wanting to shift your body to a more comfortable position, eat breakfast, or check your email. This part of your mind doesn't just experience thoughts, perceptions, and feelings but also has an intention to act. Whether subtle or strong, see if you notice a component of urge wrapped up with every moment of consciousness, without needing to act on it.

DEDICATION
Dedicate any increased awareness of your mind's mental factors to gaining more control over how you respond to objects, thoughts, and experiences in everyday life.

Experiencing consciousness

While in college during the early 1990s, I used to visit the campus bookstore each week, searching its shelves for new releases that might better explain life's mysteries. One day I was thrilled to discover a book called *Consciousness Explained* by Daniel Dennett. But after finishing its final chapter, I was left puzzled, because the book seemed to deny that my subjective conscious experience existed at all. Later, I found out that others shared my bewilderment, and today some of Dennett's critics joke that his book should have been entitled *Consciousness Explained Away.*

Denying our subjective experience seems senseless to me, because the one thing that each of us knows for certain is that we exist and we are aware. David Chalmers describes my conundrum as the "hard problem of consciousness." That is the question of how certain processes we can observe in the brain—like neurons firing and blood flowing—are related to our subjective conscious experiences of color, music, or joy.

Buddhism relies heavily on subjective experience to establish its models for consciousness, some of which I share in this section. One of the key reasons for Buddhists wanting to understand consciousness is to gain access to its subtler levels, where you discover a non-conceptual sense of who you are that lies beneath perception, thought, and even personality. You do this not just for the adventure or out of curiosity but because such knowledge can leave you with a lasting wellspring of inner happiness.

There is a concept in Mahayana Buddhism of the *continuity of mind*, a conviction that your mind has existed forever and will continue to live on forever. With this confidence comes a responsibility to evolve your ever-changing mind toward genuine happiness, wisdom, and compassion. But if you don't believe in such a vast timescale for your existence, is it still possible to conjure up the same sense of awe and responsibility in your practice? A method that has worked for me is to look at the present moment, down to its most subtle level—to have an experience of the mind *right now*, without worrying about its existence before or after that moment.

There are many ways to break through to this subtler aspect of the mind, and I share a few of them in the sections that follow, each with a guided meditation. Normally, these nature of mind practices are undertaken by advanced practitioners. However, I have found that curious, analytically minded people can respond well to these methods, often achieving powerful direct experiences of the subtle nature of the mind early in their meditation journey.

The clear and knowing mind

One Buddhist definition of the mind is that it is *clear* and *knowing*. The clarity of your mind is its ability to reflect the world as objects of consciousness. The knowing aspect of your mind is its power to understand and engage with those objects of consciousness. As you start to recognize and observe these two aspects of your mind, you become more attuned to the encompassing awareness in which both of these aspects arise.

MEDITATION ON THE CLEAR
AND KNOWING MIND

First relax into whatever passes through your mind.

Then let go of thoughts, feelings, and perceptions to notice how the nature of your mind without thoughts has a clarity to it, like the reflective face of a mirror or the transparency of a lens. As thoughts, feelings, and perceptions arise, notice how they appear like reflections or refractions within this clear mind.

Now observe the mind's knowing quality—a direct way of knowing that goes beyond labels and concepts.

Rest in these clear and knowing aspects of the mind for a moment, however you see them.

The space of your mind

Not all people think visually. But for those who do, as you experience perceptions, thoughts, and feelings, they may appear to come and go within some kind of mental space. As objects arise in this space, they may seem to emerge from some sort of mental material that they then dissolve back into, like shapes oozed out from a 3D printer then melted back down. Or objects might seem to arise instantaneously, like holographic reflections. Simply watch with an open mind and find your own metaphors for the experience.

MEDITATION ON THE SPACE
OF YOUR MIND

First relax your mind. Let your thoughts, feelings, and perceptions fade into the distance. Then steer your attention to the space in which they appear. Examine this space with curiosity and open-mindedness.

Is the space of your consciousness dim or bright?

Is it clear or obstructed?

Does it stay the same or does it change?

Does the space of your mind have a size? Is it contained within your skull, or within your whole body? Does it fill the room where you are sitting? Does your mind grow as you think about your neighborhood, your country, the planet, or even the whole universe?

Does the space of your mind overlap with other minds or does it feel separate from them?

HOW OBJECTS APPEAR IN THE SPACE OF YOUR MIND

Now watch how objects appear within the space of your mind. The signals from your eyes, ears, imagination, and memory transform into forms, sounds, and other perceptions that take shape in your awareness.

Whatever texture and color the mind has gets sculpted into the form of what you perceive. See how these mental objects rise and fall within your consciousness. You can bring each appearance closer to examine it or let it fade away.

The mind as a stream of conscious moments

Another Buddhist model of the mind describes a stream of conscious moments in which thoughts arise, take center stage, then diminish and disappear. In a variation on this, you can observe how each new moment of consciousness appears to have a duration, allowing you to split that moment in two. You can do this again and again until you either arrive at a moment of consciousness that seems indivisible or recedes into the infinitely small.

When I first learned this meditation, I was struck by its similarity to calculus, the mathematics of change. Before calculus, mathematicians were only able to approximate the area under a curve by slicing it into thin rectangles and then adding them all up. Calculus revealed that you can shrink the rectangles forever, magically adding up an infinite number of infinitely thin slices to arrive at a perfect answer.

Just like calculus, in this meditation, as you slice moments of consciousness until they are smaller and smaller, there may come a singular point where you realize that a moment is only a label imposed by your mind. Where did the past moment go? Where is the future one coming from? Does an infinitely thin slice of time have no duration? Or does it somehow become an ever-present now?

This breakthrough from logical to experiential is the essence of analytical meditation. You use a conceptual process to arrive at a non-conceptual realization about your mind and reality; in this case, that there may only be the present moment.

Meditating on the temporal aspect of the mind is a way to reason about your consciousness that can suddenly land you in a direct experience of consciousness itself. But none of this is meant to suggest that your consciousness *is* a series of time slices, just as no word is the thing it describes. Buddhism offers many paths to a direct experience of consciousness. And kids sometimes have easier access to realizations that we as adults struggle with. One night at dinner, I asked my then eight-year-old daughter what her favorite time of day was and she said, "My favorite time of the day is now, now, now, now, now, now, now …"

MEDITATION ON THE STREAM OF CONSCIOUS MOMENTS

See your mind as a stream of conscious moments.

Notice how each has a beginning that touches the past, an end that touches the future, and a middle with a duration.

Cut a moment of consciousness in half. Then slice one of its halves again. Do this again and again until you break through to a singularity of time sliced infinitely thin. Here, there is no past because it's already gone. And there is no future because it's not here yet.

Let go of your analysis and open yourself up to whatever direct experience you have, the mystery of the present moment.

The gaps between thoughts

As you watch your thoughts come and go in meditation, between the end of one and the start of the next you can sometimes become aware of a short gap when the mind is empty. These moments, when you are thinking of "nothing," are another place to discover a subtler aspect of your consciousness that is usually buried beneath stimulation, worries, and plans—a beautiful part of your mind that you rarely get to see. There, you may feel a pleasant satisfaction that is unafraid of losing anything and unattached to striving for more. It is a state of mind content simply to be alive and aware.

When I go on a meditation retreat, I sometimes experience longer stretches of this transcendent state of mind without thought. It's then that I realize I don't need anything outside myself to be happy. In fact, I'm a lot happier with fewer things—less stimulation, less interaction, even less thought— just time to go inward and experience pure awareness.

MEDITATION ON THE GAPS
BETWEEN THOUGHTS

Relax your mind and watch moments of consciousness come and go.

Try to become aware of any gaps between your thoughts.

Rest in these moments between grasping at objects and ideas to become this subtler aspect of your awareness.

RETURNING TO EVERYDAY AWARENESS

When you have finished meditating on the nature of your mind, gently steer yourself back to the everyday aspects of awareness—your senses, your body, the room, objects, and any people around you. But don't completely let go of the deeper aspects of consciousness you touched during your meditation.

Even as your mind fills with thoughts, plans, movement, and work, try to remember the subtler awareness you glimpsed that underlies ordinary experience. Remembering this subtler awareness in everyday life can bring a shimmering sense of aliveness and presence to everything you encounter.

DEDICATION
Dedicate any insights that you've had while meditating on the mind to gradually expand your awareness of the subtler aspects of your consciousness. Through the rest of your day, notice how your experience of yourself and reality changes with this deeper understanding of your mind and how it interacts with the world.

Does immaterial mean supernatural?

So far, these meditations on consciousness haven't asked (much less answered) the hard question of how consciousness relates to the brain. In Buddhism, consciousness is generally viewed as immaterial, continuing on in some form after the body dies. For scientific materialists, consciousness is a side-effect of neurons firing that disappears at the time of death. Without admitting to anything supernatural, some scientists take a position between these two extremes, saying that the information flowing through neurons does have a reality apart from those neurons. This perspective may be no different from saying that computer software is separate from computer hardware, despite its dependence on circuits and semiconductors.

I like software as an analogy for mental activity because no one debates whether software exists, yet software doesn't have a literal material form. Like thought, software is a constantly changing stream of information that flows through computer hardware, input and output devices, and the human minds perceiving and changing them. We would never say that software is merely the hardware it runs on or the memory it is stored in, but we don't get mystical and claim that software is a metaphysical phenomenon either. Software is just dynamically changing immaterial information.

The problem is that the word *immaterial* can make people uncomfortable. When we hear it, many of us assume that it refers to something religious or supernatural. But like software and information, science and psychology already accept many immaterial phenomena, though we may not realize it.

Mathematics is immaterial. From arithmetic and algebra to the equations that underpin reality, mathematics doesn't literally exist on school worksheets or in the fundamental forces of nature. Yet mathematics functions: it can solve problems, make predictions, and describe physical reality better than words. Physicist David Deutsch argues this forcefully when he says, "the laws of physics are not themselves physical objects."

On a sweeter note, we all believe in love. But love isn't material either. Where do you find love? Is it in your brain or body? Is it in a love letter or in the sound of the words "I love you?" When you blush in response to a heart emoji that pops up on your phone, is the love you feel in those red and pink pixels?

There is no such thing as a mathematics detector or a love detector, just as we don't yet have a consciousness detector. Yet we accept the existence of the immaterial phenomena of mathematics and love—not only because they are useful in understanding our world but also because they *feel* real.

So, saying that the mind has an existence apart from the brain doesn't require a supernatural belief in a soul. It merely means that the activity of the mind is not identical to the physical components of the brain. Instead, the mind's constantly changing immaterial information and the brain's hardware are interdependent in ways that we don't yet fully understand.

People sometimes use the word "spiritual" to refer to these immaterial aspects of reality, and I like this definition. When I use the word in this book, that is what I mean—defining spiritual not in any religious or supernatural sense but, instead, as the commonsense understanding that there is more to existence than material reality. If you like, call it information. We find this spiritual reality in our minds.

PART 2

STAGES OF THE PATH

5

STAGE 1:
THE PRECIOUS LIFE

It's a safe bet that if you are reading this paragraph right now, you are alive. You are also healthy enough to be awake and aware. You have a little bit of leisure time, a place to rest, and you are likely in a country where you can freely choose what to read and believe. From a Buddhist perspective, these basics may be all you need to enjoy the fruits of analytical meditation: developing your best qualities, building a life of meaningful connections, and making the world a better place. Thich Nhat Hanh expressed this beautifully when he wrote:

> Every morning when we wake up, we have twenty-four brand new hours to live. What a precious gift! We have the capacity to live in a way that these twenty-four hours will bring peace, joy, and happiness to ourselves and others.

This is the essence of the first stage in A Skeptic's Path to Enlightenment: the precious life. Billions of people aren't fortunate enough to have these basic freedoms of health, safety, and leisure. So, for those of us lucky enough to possess them, remembering this each day helps us reset our minds to realize how fortunate we are and how much good we can accomplish.

Making the most of our lives doesn't mean we need to act like superheroes. The Dalai Lama once said, "Whenever I see someone, I always smile … I think sometimes it is better to see a human smiling face rather than meditating." A simple smile and everyday kindness can have a huge positive effect on the world around us, an everyday complement to the power of meditation.

The practical benefits for your own mind of meditating on the precious life include countering hopelessness, apathy, and depression, and promoting gratitude, enthusiasm, and awe, because it is empowering to know that you may already have everything you need to achieve a happy, meaningful life.

Why is there something rather than nothing?

The traditional Buddhist approach to meditating on the precious life is to not only appreciate the profound worth of simply being alive but also to consider how this life compares to the many others that came before it. Buddhists appreciate how, after an endless chain of prior lives, their good karma has finally propelled them to a rebirth as a rational, empathetic human being instead of an instinct-driven animal, a tortured hell-being, or a pleasure-obsessed god.

But if you weren't raised Buddhist, you probably don't believe in past lives, karma, or other realms, and the logic of the lamrim's first topic doesn't make much sense. If you are a skeptic who only grounds your beliefs in what science and psychology can currently prove, Thich Nhat Hahn's words probably grab you more urgently—that each new day you're still alive is a gift. And there is the possibility of creating joy and connection in these next twenty-four hours because, whether you believe in reincarnation or not, life is precious.

In fact, it may feel even more precious to those of us who believe we have only one life to live—and not infinite future ones to try again if this one doesn't work out. I had a powerful realization in my twenties when I first came across a quote attributed to Voltaire: "It is no more surprising to be born twice than to be born once." Reading this, I awakened to the recognition that just existing at all is far more miraculous than any hypothetical possibility of existing again and again.

Gottfried Leibniz stated the fundamental question of existence even more bluntly in 1714 when he wrote, "Why is there something rather than nothing?" No one is likely to ever answer this profound question, but it is a reminder that all we have evidence for in our universe is "something."

Robert Thurman, the foremost Western scholar of Tibetan Buddhism, illuminates this existential truth when he says wryly, "The idea that nothing is something is simply irrational. Nothing is a word that has no reference. It's just a negation. It means something that isn't there."

The definition of "nothing" is nonexistence. All anyone has ever observed is something. So another point in this first stage of the precious life is to feel how miraculous it is to be part of the only "something" that any of us know of: life on our planet in all its glorious diversity.

The scientific miracle of life

For a long time, I struggled to find a scientific analog for the natural sense of awe and responsibility a Buddhist feels in the face of infinite past and future lives. Is it possible for a skeptic to feel the same sense of awe about a finite life?

I eventually discovered a sense of wonder that expands on Leibniz's existential mystery by reflecting on the scientific origins of life. As a boy growing up in the 1980s, I couldn't get enough of a TV show called *Cosmos*, hosted by the eminent astronomer Carl Sagan. He gave me my first sense of the vastness of a universe that seemed more awesome than any religious creation story. When Sagan intoned his tagline, "Billions and billions ... ," I got the shivers, as he went on to tell a tale of an impossibly old universe that ends at a minuscule stretch of history in which we humans have at last evolved the capacity to know, think, and feel.

Cosmos introduced the "cosmic calendar," which compresses the entire 13.8 billion years of our universe down into one Earth year—a clever device that helps our human minds comprehend the newness of our species. On this calendar, a single day is 38 million years of our universe's existence, and a second is 500 years. The big bang occurs in the first nanosecond of January 1 and the present moment is the last instant of December 31.

From January to September, the universe evolves over
9 billion years until our star and solar system finally form
from the debris of earlier stellar explosions. All the Earth's
heavy elements, including the building blocks of life, came
from those stars that exploded before ours even formed.

Soon after the Earth's formation, simple life appeared,
3.8 billion years ago. Three more months pass on the cosmic
calendar—which is another 3.6 billion years—until dinosaurs
show up and live for just one calendar day. Mammals emerge
the next day (another 38 million years of universe time) and
gradually evolve into monkeys, apes, and early hominids.

Modern humans show up late to the party, on New Year's
Eve, December 31 at 11:52PM, only 200,000 years ago in real
time. And recorded history, starting 12,000 years ago, begins
at 11:59PM and 33 seconds. The cosmic calendar's final second
holds all the past 500 years of modern civilization, from
Leonardo da Vinci to the Internet.

So far, everything we currently know about the universe's
evolution says that it took 13.8 billion years for humanity
to emerge. And out of 100 billion stars in our galaxy and a
100 billion other galaxies, we have yet to find evidence of
other creative, rational beings like us. Carl Sagan poetically
proclaims, "We are a way for the cosmos to know itself"—that
humanity's formidable role in the universe may be to serve as
its mind.

I now lead meditations in this more scientific way,
according to these profound facts that awed me as a boy,
reflecting not only on the cosmic evolution of galaxies, stars,
planets, and life but also on our remarkable intelligence
and compassion. Every once in a while, you may reflect on
the marvel of the universe and your miraculous place in it.
But what happens when you do this every day, grounding
yourself in the wonder of "Why is there something rather
than nothing?"

Bringing Carl Sagan's famous quote down to everyday
reality, *you are a way to know yourself.* And maybe this is the

great responsibility of a human life: to become genuinely aware of your place in the universe at the end of 13.8 billion years of cosmic evolution—and to make the most of it.

What's the first thing you do when you wake up in the morning?

A more grounding approach to appreciating your precious life is to ask, "What's the first thing I do when I wake up in the morning?" Today, most of us check our phones. And for a lot of us, this is not a matter of urgently helping humanity or gently pressing play for a guided meditation. We check the news, social media, sports, stocks, or work.

When I dive into these distracting activities before meditating, my compulsions and fears can dominate the rest of the day. I find it hard to shake off the chain of mindless impulses that follows from a day that starts off indulging my hunger for information, entertainment, or praise.

But when I start the day quietly, getting to know my own thoughts, experiencing the simple beauty of awareness, steering my mind toward stability and satisfaction, and setting a motivation to make the day meaningful, I find that I am more present. I connect more easily with others. And I make choices that I'm proud of.

A powerful morning ritual in the Tibetan tradition is to recall your great fortune in having one more day on this Earth. As soon as you wake up, you think, "I am alive. I made it through the night. Life comes with no guarantee, and many people died yesterday, from accidents, illness, violence, or old age." With this sobering view in mind, you set an intention to make the most of your day.

Seeing the briefness of your life helps cast off pettiness, mindlessness, and compulsive behavior. And thoughts of our shared fragility can help you to meet peoples' gazes with affection and respect, and to pursue actions that genuinely benefit yourself and others.

If you have some safety and security, if you are lucky enough to have a job and money in the bank, then maybe you already have everything you need for a happy life. And the fact that you've explored books and teachings about self-reflection becomes the basis for the tremendous adventure you embark on in analytical meditation: to transcend the mundane mechanics of everyday life, become self-aware, and gain control of your mind. It's worth making the small effort each morning to dive into your mind for a few minutes, to see who you are beneath thoughts and stimulation, and create the causes for genuine happiness by simply being present and aware.

Gratitude like this can seem sappy to those of us raised in a culture of ironic detachment, but gratitude is one of the most researched practices of positive psychology, associated with well-established beneficial outcomes. In studies of people who practice gratitude regularly, participants experienced greater happiness, more positive emotions, increased resilience, better health, and stronger relationships.

Analytical meditation on the precious life is a specific type of gratitude practice that helps you ground your day in the rarity and awe of your place in the universe—and a wish to make the most of it.

Why we don't seize the day

I want to acknowledge that cultivating a reverence for simply having another day alive might seem indulgent to someone who is trying to slog through a life that feels lonely, painful, or unjust. You might not feel that you have the luxury of savoring life's philosophical value as you struggle to pay the rent, endure an angry boss, mourn a break-up, or suffer illness, inequity, or any of life's other stresses. I have had stretches of life like this, when problems pile on top of problems. And you may be enduring such a time in your life right now.

But even if your own life is okay at the moment, how can you selfishly treasure twenty-four hours of safety and peace when billions of others suffer from poverty, illness, famine, war, and injustice? Not everyone has the opportunity for peaceful self-reflection. And many people live in countries where they are not permitted to freely study and discuss the ideas you're reading about right now. Is it really appropriate to chill out in meditation and appreciate the beauty of a safe, privileged life?

Your upbringing can also become an obstacle to appreciating your life's precious opportunities. Many of us were raised with values like "Boys don't cry" or "Be a good girl" that seal off our ability to express—or even know—what we are thinking and feeling.

You may also fail to appreciate the potential in every moment when your powerful primitive brain takes hold of your mind and body. This instinctual part of yourself is genetically adapted to the hunt-and-kill savannas our ancestors evolved in, which hardly bears any resemblance to our safer modern world of supermarkets and smartphones. When someone cuts in front of you at the store, or when your boss says the work you did was only "okay," those old instinctual ego-driven forces can make you feel just as threatened as you would if you had been attacked by a tiger, and cause you to lash out in anger or freeze in fear.

Your primitive mind can also drive you to compulsively seek pleasure: to excessively eat, drink, or take drugs; to mindlessly chase bodily pleasure in your next sexual partner or physical thrill; or to relentlessly pursue your next deal or promotion. And I share these insights from personal experience. They are all ways that we can grope mindlessly through life without appreciating its opportunities.

But even if you are fortunate enough to be free from the harsh difficulties of poverty, war, oppression, addiction, severe illness, or chronic pain, you may still lack something that is critical to making your life meaningful right now.

That is because many of us still fail to find the interest and time for self-reflection. This is the final obstacle to achieving a meaningful life of happiness and connection. Even with sufficient money, relative health, a safe home, and a bit of free time, many of us fill it with the endless array of entertainments available to us. Or we are driven to work through evenings and weekends instead of simply enjoying being alive and aware in the company of people we love.

In a life free from the worst forms of suffering, one of the most disheartening situations to end up in is to have found an interest in life's deepest questions, but then to never take the time to explore them; never make the effort to become educated about the true keys to a happy, purposeful life. That is why the Buddhist definition of a precious life is for us to not only be healthy, intelligent human beings, living in a safe place with a modest level of resources, but also for us to have the interest and the inner drive to seriously probe the mysteries of existence.

MEDITATION ON THE PRECIOUS LIFE

Meditating on the precious life helps us feel awe toward our place in the universe, urgency in the face of our short life, and enthusiasm for the opportunities we find in every new day.

PRELIMINARIES
Start with the preliminaries of posture, motivation, refuge, and stabilizing on the breath.

In your motivation, if you aren't just waking up, you can imagine that you are and think, "I'm so grateful to have another day of life, to have this body, a safe place to sleep, a modest amount of comfort and security, family and friends. Maybe I have everything I need to be happy.

There's nothing better I could be doing with these few minutes right now than going inward to understand who I am beneath stimulation, stress, entertainment, and thoughts; getting to know the deep core of my awareness to explore the mystery of being alive and aware right now."

THE PRECIOUS LIFE

In meditating on the precious life, you reflect on your good fortune. Of course, you face many hardships too. But, for a moment, practice gratitude for whatever you have: for simply being alive and aware; for your body and its senses, through which you can appreciate the beauty of the world; for whatever resources you have: food, shelter, safety, security, health, education, work, family and friends.

Then, feel gratitude that you have found an interest in going beyond striving, beyond competitiveness, beyond entertainment. There is a place for all these things in life, but there's also something more. Feel grateful that you have been exposed to ideas, teachers, and friends who value inner happiness, who contemplate the worth of an existence that rises above material accumulation.

Feel grateful that you are not only curious and interested in finding the deepest sources of life's meaning but also have made an effort to pursue self-awareness, to read books, listen to teachers, and go on an inner adventure through meditation; to probe in an honest way what's inside your mind and discover how to be happy, and how to be of genuine benefit to others.

Feel gratitude if you have the basics of life that many can't take for granted: those people experiencing poverty, illness, war, natural disasters, political, racial, or gender oppression, and those afflicted by unquenchable addictions to food, sex, drugs, power, fame, or wealth.

Maybe you have everything you need to be happy. And all you need is to make the effort to live this day aware of your precious life, remembering everything that you are grateful for.

THE SCIENTIFIC MIRACLE OF LIFE

Now contemplate your connection to the universe. You sit in the center of a universe 13.8 billion years old with 100 billion galaxies. There are at least 100 billion planets in our own galaxy, the Milky Way; an estimated 100 million of them with rocky planets like ours circling their own burning star. One of them is our own sun, 4.5 billion years old, where life on its third planet, the Earth, has existed for at least 3 billion years. Over that time, the scientific magic of evolution transformed simple chemicals into cells, worms, fish, snakes, dinosaurs, mammals, and monkeys. Humanity arrives at the tip of history, only 200,000 years ago. Some 10,000 generations of humans pass by—so many of them struggling, dying at birth, hungry, violent, afraid.

And then you are born.

Now, despite its drawbacks, discomforts, and injustices, you are lucky enough to live in a world that is safer and more abundant for humans than it has ever been before.

There is no evidence yet for any other life in the universe. What if humanity is the pinnacle of cosmic evolution, the sole way for the universe to know itself? If being intelligent and self-aware is unfathomably rare and precious, how should you spend your day? What is the best way to achieve a happy mind, and to live with dignity, meaning, and connection?

It may be nothing more than what you are doing right now: going inward, probing your mind, cultivating the true causes of happiness in the present moment through gratitude and self-awareness. Soon you will go out into your day to deepen your connections with others, and make our fragile, beautiful world a little bit better for everyone else who shares it.

Rest in these thoughts for a minute, in your profound connection to all the universe and all of history, your gratefulness for being alive. How will you make the most of this day?

6

STAGE 2: EMBRACING IMPERMANENCE

I once heard someone ask Stephen King what people are most afraid of and his answer surprised me. The most successful horror writer of all time didn't say serial killers, drowning, or cancer. He didn't even say death. He said people's greatest fear is change.

One of the biggest paradoxes of Buddhism is its claim that reflecting on the certainty of things falling apart is a path to a happy, peaceful mind. The first time I heard this was the day after the terrorist attacks of September 11, 2001. I was in Boston visiting my brother, and his teacher, Geshe Tsulga, offered to give a lecture for people grieving over the tragedy. I had only been studying Buddhism for a year, and I found myself surprised that this great Tibetan lama didn't focus on mindfulness or compassion—the two Buddhist topics Westerners seem to find most helpful. Instead, he spoke almost solely about impermanence.

Geshe Tsulga began by saying how none of us imagined that these buildings would collapse—not today, not in a hundred years. If we really examined our minds, we had probably assumed that they would stand forever. And yet these buildings did fall, killing many innocent people as they collapsed. He invited us to open our hearts to those suffering, and to the fear that many of us were experiencing. But he also said what happened was an important reminder that nothing is certain and everything is always changing. Any one of us could have been in that building the previous day. And each of us could die tomorrow. Knowing that, how do we want to live our lives today? And are the ways that we spend our time and the goals that we pursue truly the most meaningful?

With such a charged introduction to the topic, I found it hard not to take Geshe Tsulga's advice to start meditating on impermanence. Later, when I began teaching meditation, I discovered that this topic often resonated with many students more than any other. Eventually it became the first practice I would share with someone who had never tried meditation, because meditating on impermanence requires no belief. It's a clear-eyed look at reality that gives your life greater purpose and urgency.

We've all experienced big jolts of change: a financial crisis, the start of a war, an untimely death. Moments like these usually shock us. But if you observe those who have meditated on impermanence for years, not only are they unsurprised at times like these but they are also immediately ready to help in whatever ways they can.

In our personal lives, understanding impermanence helps when we experience job loss, break-ups, or sudden illness, because it reminds us that the most difficult problems we face are themselves subject to change. And in the face of huge challenges like social injustice, war, and climate change, impermanence gives us courage when we realize that these issues, too, are not as static and hopeless as they appear.

But meditating on impermanence isn't just a medicine we take to help us face up to difficult moments. It also promotes gratitude, resilience, and courage in our everyday lives. It helps us to find joy in how things really are rather than feeling the pain of how we wish them to be. It helps us to realize that change is not only possible but is also a truth that pervades all reality. Knowing this, we can both accept the inevitability of change and become agents of change who positively transform the world.

The arc of change

When meditating on impermanence, you start with the big, recognizable ways that things change: bombs fall, diseases spread, and relationships end. But wars also cease, the sick recover, and people fall in love.

Through impermanence, you learn to see an object not simply as it appears at this moment but along its entire arc of existence, from its inception to its demise. Consider the place where you live—perhaps where you're sitting right now. It was conceived, planned, and built by dozens of people, at great cost, over the course of years. And, eventually, it will be gone. It could slowly crumble or suddenly burn, flood, or collapse. When you walk down the street, you can look at each structure you pass and imagine the day someone thought to build there, the cost and effort of construction, and the moment that building will fall, whether tomorrow or centuries from now.

Everything you buy with your hard-earned money— phones, clothes, and cars—these, too, will all eventually wear out, get lost or stolen, or you may simply tire of them. When you purchase a new smartphone, you usually don't consider how you will feel about it in a few years' time, when it will be slow and scratched and you'll again want something new. The next time you are about to buy a new one, try to picture the day it will become so old and worn out that you replace it too.

And whether you love or hate your government's leaders, they are already on their way out. Someone in power may have soaring popularity today, but then tumble from office tomorrow, whether through a vote, scandal, revolution, or death. For decades Saddam Hussein ruled Iraq like a king. But once his regime was overthrown, he became a wanted fugitive, eventually found starving and sick, cowering in a hole.

Societies and civilizations also change—faster than you might think—because the average civilization lasts only about 350 years. It's sobering to realize that just as the Roman, Egyptian, and Aztec civilizations ended, today's civilizations will also inevitably collapse, either slowly through gentle evolution or quickly through conquest, revolt, or disaster. When I worry about the small losses and problems in my own life, I sometimes come back to this overarching truth that our civilization itself is finite and will one day crumble too.

Subtle change

Part of why impermanence is such a good topic for modern meditators is because today we understand the invisible levels of change in physical reality far better than we did 2,500 years ago.

From the perspective of chemistry, matter isn't solid and unchanging but made of molecules that constantly combine, divide, and dissolve. Those molecules' atoms vibrate invisibly as probabilistic clouds of buzzing subatomic particles. And, according to some interpretations, 99.99 percent of what we call "matter" is empty space. In these subtle and strange ways, change is matter's fundamental nature.

Change in your body and mind

The constant change in your body is the most intimate form of change, but even your beating heart is something you may rarely notice. Try to pay attention to it now. Put your palm on your chest to feel your heartbeat: continual change at the core of your existence. The blood it pumps courses through your veins, circling your entire body once a minute. Breath flows in and out of your lungs. Nerve impulses zip between your fingertips and brain.

Your body's living organs constantly move, process, and transform. Millions of your body's cells die every second, replaced by millions newly born. Cells are packed with frantically jostling molecules. And, like non-living matter, your body at its most fundamental level is a buzz of subatomic particles.

Heraclitus famously said that just as you never step in the same river twice, you are never the same you twice. But we now know this isn't just a metaphor. Over the course of a single year, 98 percent of all the atoms in your body are exchanged. So, even from the perspective of physics, on each birthday, you literally are a different person from the one who celebrated it last.

The conscious world of your mind is also constantly changing. Your mind moves through many mental states in a day—sometimes every few seconds. You can feel happy then quickly become sad. You can be mired in regrets from long ago, then get swept up in exciting plans for the future. You can be filled with love for your partner then, moments later, become angry or resentful. And when you probe the subtlest level of your mind, just like matter, mental events also break down into minute temporal parts.

Everyone walks the hero's journey

From Jesus Christ to Luke Skywalker, the hero's journey is a universal structure for mythical tales of growth and adventure. But each of us is also the hero of our own life. We may rarely acknowledge it, but each of us was born and every one of us will die. In between, we all experience our own struggles, conflicts, triumphs, and loves.

As you encounter people in your daily life, a powerful meditation on impermanence is to picture the moment each one of them was born. Imagine their mother's pain, her exhaustion and joy at creating a fragile new being whose life depends on her. Then, try to imagine how that person will eventually die—alone or surrounded by loved ones, agitated or at peace. This technique is especially helpful when you are angry with someone because it helps put your dispute in perspective. Picture the end of that person's life: in a hospital bed or at home, after a life that was long or short, a life of virtue or misbehavior, a life ending among friends or silently alone. Then try to imagine where that person is right now on their journey from cradle to grave: what dreams, goals, and disappointments they may have had, moments of loneliness and intimacy.

Without this kind of reflection, the people around you can seem like video game characters—mere obstacles or aids to your life's agenda. Such a rigid, self-centered view of the people around you is disconnecting and inaccurate. They are all constantly changing and each of them treasures their precious lives just as much as you do yours. Each of them lives an epic hero's journey.

Every moment is new

Accepting change also opens up all kinds of possibilities. "Every moment is new" is one of the most powerful Buddhist teachings I have ever received. I am not the same person I was yesterday. Though it may *feel* like the same conflict or craving, this moment is new, and I have the chance to act and respond differently today.

But even though all these arguments make sense logically, our habitual ways of seeing make us cling to things as though they won't change, mistakenly thinking our partner will always delight us, a seductive object will always be pleasing, or an irritating person will always make us angry.

We can cling to discouraging thoughts about ourselves like, "I'm an angry person" or "I'm an imposter," or positive thoughts like "I'm a kind person," but the only accurate statement about our thoughts and feelings is that they temporarily pass through us. We are not those thoughts and feelings. We can feel anger, love, pride, or shame. But those feelings are impermanent too.

Years after hearing Geshe Tsulga's lesson, I can now say that the practice of impermanence has helped me through many of my life's worst conflicts and calamities. I remember accepting when the powerful attraction my ex-partner and I felt for each other dissolved as our relationship came to an end. I remember letting go of despair at losing everything in a financial disaster by realizing my tragedy had the capacity to change—and that the most likely direction to go from the bottom was up, however slowly. I remember seeing how needlessly I'd held on to a lifelong grudge against my father, when measured against the briefness of life and the treasure of our relationship—and being able to finally let it go.

We don't know for sure how things will change, but we can be certain that they will. In Buddhism this isn't seen as a religious truism, but as an empirically verifiable fact. Everything we know in the universe is impermanent: our bodies, our possessions, the environment, relationships, feelings, thoughts, and plans.

When you understand impermanence, you become more capable of consciously seizing opportunities, letting go of conflicts, and overcoming grief. You open yourself to the power in the present moment and become more skilled at deeply connecting with yourself and with others. The huge global challenges we face today, of injustice, inequity, and climate change, can sometimes make us feel hopeless, but you can use the proven tool of impermanence to steer your mind away from fear and anxiety and toward confident presence and purposeful action. Impermanence reveals that even as a situation feels most desperate, often that is when things start to improve, as the world naturally swings through extremes and people turn their efforts toward solutions.

MEDITATION ON IMPERMANENCE

PRELIMINARIES

Perform the preliminaries of posture, motivation, refuge, and stabilizing on the breath. In your motivation, you can feel confident that your good qualities are your natural, deepest ones; that disturbing thoughts and emotions are transitory; that your mind is trainable; and that, through meditation, you can gradually allow your natural kindness, warmth, and generosity to shine through.

THE IMPERMANENCE OF THE BODY

Become aware of your body. Think of its parts one by one: your feet, legs, hands, arms, torso, neck, head, eyes, mouth, nose, ears, and your skin—the boundary between you and the world.

Begin to feel the momentary changes in your body: your heart beating, blood coursing through your veins, breath flowing in and out of your lungs, nerve impulses zipping from the tips of your fingers and toes, up to your brain and back.

Try to imagine the subtler cellular changes in your body's trillions of living cells: blood, skin, stomach, and brain cells, moving, changing, reproducing; the millions of your body's cells dying every second, replaced by millions newly born.

Each of these cells is also made of countless parts: atoms and their subatomic particles, clouds of energy vibrating and colliding.

THE IMPERMANENCE OF THE MIND

Now turn your attention to your mind, constantly filled with fresh thoughts, perceptions, feelings, memories, plans, fears, and desires. For a minute, watch your mind from a distance, without trying to control your thoughts. Notice how new thoughts appear and disappear. Observe and label them without becoming attached to them, and without pushing them away.

THE IMPERMANENCE OF THE OUTER WORLD

Picture the world immediately surrounding you—the cushion you are seated on, the walls and ceiling, the furniture, and the surrounding space. Imagine them the way science tells us they exist—buzzing clouds of energetic particles that your senses mistake as solid forms.

Think of all your possessions: your clothes, your phone, your car, and your home (if you are lucky enough to have them). Each of these is subject to change. Nothing lasts forever. Visualize them old, faded, worn out, destroyed: your house torn down, your car a crushed metal cube, your phone recycled, your clothes worn to rags. How do your feelings about them change?

Even when objects manage to last a lifetime, you can still grow tired of them, give them away, or pack them up in a box that you forget about for the rest of your life.

Then remember how impermanence doesn't only manifest when things wear out, when they are destroyed, or when you grow tired of them, but is something that happens at every instant, in the subtle changes to objects' molecules, atoms, and subatomic particles.

THE IMPERMANENCE OF PEOPLE AND RELATIONSHIPS

Now bring to mind the people around you: family, friends, acquaintances, strangers you pass on the street or in stores. Each of them was born. Imagine the profound moment their mother gave birth. And each of them will die. Imagine them on their deathbed, alone or surrounded by loved ones. At this moment they are constantly changing, too, just like your own body and mind.

Your friendships, romantic partners, and work relationships are all also in flux. Recall friends and romantic partners who were once the most important people in your life, yet are now distant acquaintances or even enemies. Relationships can end due to conflicts, revelations, or distance. You can grow tired or bored, or simply drift apart from the people who once brought you so much joy.

But also, somewhere out there in the world, alive and breathing right now, there may be a stranger who will become your dearest friend, your wisest teacher, or an intimate partner for the rest of your life.

CHANGE MEANS FLUIDITY

Quietly contemplate impermanence for a moment. Let anything come to mind—objects, people, relationships; your body, your mind; thoughts, regrets, plans; politicians, climate change, social injustice; even civilization itself. Apply the logic of impermanence to each of them. When you glimpse a clear, strong sense of the ever-changing nature of any one of these, let go of the analysis and stay with your experience that transcends words.

Then, when it inevitably fades, analyze the impermanence of your body, mind, or another object intellectually. When the sense of impermanence returns, release yourself into it again.

Remember that whatever is unpleasant or disturbing won't last forever. It might even change for the better. And whatever is beautiful or pleasing will also eventually change or disappear, so it can't offer lasting happiness. Yet still life keeps presenting new impermanent opportunities for beauty, meaning, and connection.

DEDICATION

May whatever progress you've made toward seeing the impermanent nature of reality carry into your day. When you enjoy something pleasurable—a delicious meal, a walk in the woods, the touch of your partner—see if you can be fully present for it. You won't always experience such pleasures; this might even be the last time you do.

See if you can enjoy without clinging, without yearning for a next time. So often your appreciation of life's riches is ruined by plotting the next time you'll get it or worrying that you'll never have it again.

When you recognize that external things can't give you lasting happiness and satisfaction, your attachment to them lessens, but your enjoyment of them may increase. The Mahayana Buddhist view is that by realizing the impermanent nature of pleasure, you can then appreciate it even more. Without unrealistically wishing for pleasure to last forever or yearning for it to repeat again and again, you can enjoy it fully and immediately as it truly is—impermanent.

7

STAGE 3: MENTAL CAUSE AND EFFECT

There is an incredible moment in a movie called *The Tree of Life*, when a grief-stricken mother is praying to God, begging to understand her young son's senseless death. Suddenly, the film cuts to a scene 13.8 billion years earlier, to witness the big bang.

Slowly, we watch the whole universe unfold—nebulae coalescing, stars forming, planets fusing, then a lightning strike that sparks life on Earth, which starts to evolve. We slow down and zoom in to a riverside 70 million years ago, where an angry velociraptor is about to kill a gentler plant-eating dinosaur. Somehow, the predator has second thoughts and walks away from its chance to kill, in what looks like the first moment of mercy on our planet.

But then this compassionate dinosaur looks up to watch an asteroid streak through the atmosphere, which kills it and most of life on Earth. Eventually, we arrive back at the present time, with this epic flashback having given us the answer to the mother's question of why her son died, an answer that required recapitulating all of history itself.

What I think the movie's director Terrence Malick suggests in this magnificent sequence is that everything in the universe is interconnected in an endless chain of cause and effect. When we ask why something happens, we come to realize that everything affects everything else, back to the very dawn of time.

In the search for the cause and effect in our own lives, we may need to take a similar journey backward, looking at how our minds have been affected by our parents, our culture, our education, the media, evolution, and even, like the awe-inspiring rewind in *The Tree of Life*, the unfolding of the universe itself.

Karma, destiny, or randomness?

For millennia, people have asked the vexing question, "Why do bad things happen in the world?" The answer given in Buddhism is *karma*—an invisible force of nature governing the urges that pop into our minds. You will recall from chapter 4 that urge is one of five ever-present mental factors. We don't always act on these urges but, when we do, the Buddhist view is that our actions will be either constructive or destructive, sowing the seeds for later happiness or unhappiness.

So far, the Buddhist view of cause and effect sounds similar to the results of neuroscientific research, which show that each of our thoughts and actions creates future propensities for similar thoughts and actions: "Neurons that fire together, wire together." But karma in Buddhism goes further than thought conditioning to explain that external events like accidents, sickness, and poverty also occur due to people's forgotten bad deeds from prior lives. Karma is seen as a force as real as gravity that affects both matter and mind and requires multiple lifetimes to explain why bad things happen to good people.

This is not to say that karma couldn't possibly be true. We lack firm explanations for why many things occur in the universe, and karma offers an answer to compete with God's will, luck, or randomness. However, karma has not been proven to be true using the scientific method and it might never allow for the kind of experimental evaluation that science demands to firmly prove or disprove it.

Interestingly, determinism—the idea that there is a predestined path from the big bang to every action occurring right now, is about as controversial as karma is to today's scientists. Einstein believed in a predictable universe, perhaps like Terrence Malick's epic rewind, but Einstein lost his argument to quantum theorists. Today, most physicists believe that randomness, not determinism, is at the root of the universe. Yet, even if determinism were true, would it be any more comforting to throw up our hands and say "big bang" instead of " karma" when something takes us by surprise?

Though we can't predict, much less control, the vast array of events surrounding us, the compassionate dinosaur in *The Tree of Life* hints at the practical application of cause and effect—that it is possible for us to control our minds. Regardless of whether you believe in karma or not, what Buddhism offers are specific methods to gain conscious control over *mental* cause and effect: ways to steer our minds toward thoughts and actions that benefit ourselves and others, that lead to a life of meaning and connection—and even to a better world.

Psychological karma

In the book *Samsara, Nirvana, and Buddha Nature*, His Holiness the Dalai Lama makes some clarifying statements about how karma in Buddhism relates to the scientific view of cause and effect. To summarize, His Holiness says that he believes events in the natural universe are controlled by the laws of physics, as science today understands them. But mental events—how people act, react, and make decisions—are governed more by internal karmic and psychological laws than physical forces and particles: "Karma enters the picture when sentient beings' intentions and their happiness and suffering are involved."

Buddhist morality emerges from this understanding of mental cause and effect. We want to be happy, and we don't want to suffer. Some actions lead to happiness, while others lead to suffering. Like other religions and ethical frameworks, Buddhism shares more or less the same list of non-virtues (or "sins") that lead to suffering: killing, stealing, sexual misconduct, lying, and so forth. But the logic of *why* these are non-virtues lies in the fact that our actions not only inflict pain on others but also inflict lasting psychological pain on *ourselves*. Fundamentally, harming others hurts us, too, disturbing our minds so that it becomes difficult for us to feel happy. And healing this pain requires both making amends to those we've hurt and some inner processing.

The role of ethics in human behavior is now increasingly acknowledged by science, too, recognizing that we evolved as social beings who care about those around us and feel compassion when others are distressed. There is more and more scientific validation of altruistic behavior in both animals and people that shows how this seemingly noble state of mind is evolutionarily advantageous for sustaining a species, because communities of mutual support generally fare much better than those composed of selfish individuals.

This is one explanation for why we feel good when we help one another and feel bad when we harm others: evolution may have a karma-like bias that rewards prosocial behavior. Robert Thurman puts this poetically when he points to the abundant living planet we live on and says that the universe is biased toward connection and away from disconnection. Caring for our planet and helping other beings are acts of connection, while poisoning our environment or taking someone's life are acts of disconnection.

The Buddhist viewpoint is that an important way to maintain this connection to ourselves and to others is through specific meditations that help us to let go of our regrets and enrich our capacity to do good. Without such daily practices, the small and large misdeeds of life can fester and grow, negatively affecting our behavior. We compulsively lash out or withdraw. Even our perception of the world changes: kind words can sound critical when we are in a foul mood, and formerly pleasurable experiences stop bringing us joy. Before podcasts and playlists, I used to listen to the radio in the car, and I noticed how, on some days, every song sounded terrible. Then, the next day, suddenly every song sounded great again. Eventually I realized that it wasn't the songs that were changing, but my mood. My attitude toward the world changed how I perceived it.

Consciously or unconsciously, we know how our actions make us feel inside. We feel wholesome and at ease when we act with kindness and generosity. And we feel anxious and angry when we act harshly and selfishly. It's useful to pay attention to which actions lead us to experience positive and negative states of mind and, once we figure it out, to cultivate those actions that lead to contentment and joy.

There are many meditative approaches to gaining control over cause and effect in your own mind, steering it toward happiness and self-respect. In a way, this is the point of the entire Buddhist path. One specific method that works in everyday life is the combined practice of mindfulness and compassion. Another lesser-known method is a daily practice of rejoicing and self-forgiveness. Both are practical, non-religious ways to evaluate and process your actions each day that don't require belief in invisible karmic forces.

Mindfulness and compassion

A powerful method that can be used to treat problems in real time is the combined practice of mindfulness and compassion. Through mindfulness, you become aware of your feelings and reactive urges in a given situation. This allows you to stop before you compulsively act on a trigger, and consciously choose your response. The skill needed to stay mindfully aware is built up slowly by watching your mind and labeling its states during meditation, when there is little stimulation or conflict.

Once you've managed to become aware of your feelings before acting on them, then, through compassion, you can choose the most beneficial way to respond. Chapter 11 shares several meditations on compassion, but one simple approach is to rehearse healthy ways to respond to your triggers. In your imagination, you play through a scenario over and over, responding in the way that you'd prefer. This builds a new, more helpful habit that you later act out with your speech and body when the trigger again occurs.

To give an example from my own life, I imagine my partner acting irritable or distant, and then, instead of getting annoyed, I ask, "What's going on for you right now?" With one sentence, I have altered the chain of cause and effect that might have led us to have an argument and, instead, invited her to share her own cause and effect.

Even more powerful can be to try to understand the endless chain of cause and effect that led to the negative actions of a partner, parent, boss, politician, or anyone else. Both biology and conditioning have a huge impact on people's actions. How did their parents treat them? How did their parents treat each other? What did they learn from school, work, and the thousands of movies and TV programs they've watched since childhood? How did their nervous systems evolve over millions of years to perceive small slights to be as dangerous as a charging lion?

You can even think beyond annoying behavior to broader questions about cause and effect in the world. How did forces set in motion long ago determine who gets a disease and who doesn't, which communities will be struck by disasters, who grows wealthy, who's born poor, who gets elected, and who is subject to the world's many injustices? How much of it has anything to do with what is happening in the present moment? How much of it is under your control?

With sustained practice, an increased understanding of cause and effect helps you to realize that getting angry at someone for harming you is just as illogical as getting angry at gravity when you fall down. By learning how to understand and change your own behavior, you see that there is a longer chain of cause and effect behind everyone's habits that has little to do with the immediate face-to-face conflict in which you find yourself. With practice, forgiveness of yourself and others starts to come more naturally, because you see that people's harmful actions don't generally stem from outright hostility but, rather, from an endless chain of causes and conditions.

MEDITATION ON COMPASSIONATE CAUSE AND EFFECT

Bring to mind someone who hurt you or whose actions annoy you. It makes sense to stay away from anyone who has seriously harmed you, and even to seek protection and justice through the workplace or the law. But most of the harms we experience day to day are smaller ones that we can process in meditation, because the things people do that make us upset often have little to do with us.

Try to see the cause and effect behind this person's behavior. Even at their angriest, people who harm act from a wish to be happy. They just have a misguided view of the causes of happiness, so their actions don't end up making them happy, but only fill them with more pain. See if you can wish them happiness and mental stability. If they were genuinely happy, they'd likely stop harming you and everyone else.

Imagine how the world would be a better place if everyone—even your enemies—had what they needed: health, safety, wealth, affection, control over their mind. What would the world look like if everyone gained the wisdom to act in ways that create the true causes of happiness for themselves and for others?

Self-control and self-acceptance
In Buddhism, self-control is seen as the key to creating the causes of happiness and letting go of the causes of unhappiness, and it advances in levels, starting first with controlling our

body. Most of us mastered an aspect of this first level as a child: when we feel pain or don't get what we want, we can suppress the urge to lash out with physical violence.

The next level of self-control is verbal, which most of us have some degree of mastery over, too, albeit incomplete. Even on my best days, I say a few thoughtless things that I regret. I hurt others in small and not-so-small ways, sometimes accidentally, but often out of carelessness, self-centeredness, or unprocessed pain. Sometimes I'm surprised by how strongly I respond to a tiny slight. But I came to understand this better when I heard psychologist Bessel van der Kolk say, "There is no such thing as an overreaction." He went on to explain that we are simply responding to events other than those we are presented with, reacting to past pain or trauma that we haven't fully processed.

After taming body and speech comes level three: gaining control over the mind, which is far more difficult than the previous two. The Buddhist tradition explains that even highly realized beings still have thoughts of anger and desire, but they let those thoughts pass by without grasping on to them, acting on them, or judging themselves. Those who have mastered mindfulness are able to see disturbing thoughts as separate from the mind observing them and let unwanted emotions simply fade away without causing harm to themselves or others.

I find this view of self-acceptance quite profound. It enables us to accept whatever thoughts pass through our mind without letting them take control of our body and speech, where they do so much harm.

A daily practice of self-forgiveness

The meditation on cause and effect that I share next offers a practical method for processing our everyday harmful actions. From time to time we speak falsely, harshly, divisively, or irresponsibly. And though most of us as adults are not physically violent, we still cause bodily harm to both ourselves and others through harsh facial expressions, physical intimidation, overindulging in food or substances, or degrading our environment. In the course of our day, we may defend our actions internally. But if we look closely at our mind, each of these disconnecting acts leaves us with a feeling of disappointment in ourselves that can grow into self-loathing.

When I look back at the events I most regret in life, they are things that I said or did unthinkingly, spitefully, out of anger or pain; acts that caused others harm and sometimes even destroyed a good relationship. You may feel the same way. What do we do with the shame and guilt that we feel when we've hurt someone? We may defend our actions to others. Our friends might even reassure us that what we did was justified. But deep down, we know what we did was wrong and the pain of hurting another person lingers.

That is when the Buddhist psychological approach to cause and effect is useful. When my Tibetan teacher Geshe Dakpa was teaching us the techniques for clearing away the psychological pain of past misdeeds, he said the first step toward processing each day's wrongs is sincere regret. I asked him, "What's the difference between regret and guilt?" And he gave a simple answer: regret is honestly acknowledging that something you did was harmful and sincerely wishing not to do it again, while guilt is thinking that you are a bad person, judging or even hating yourself for having done something wrong.

Whenever I've done something that I wish I hadn't, I think about Geshe Dakpa's words. Of course, my guilt and shame don't immediately clear away. But once the first wave of strong emotion diminishes, in the quiet time before bed, I find it possible to make an honest catalog of the actions I regret from the day and rehearse what I would have preferred to have said or done instead.

When I first started leading the meditation on processing the day's misdeeds that follows, I found that, for some people who are already critical of themselves, the meditation could bring them down further instead of offering a healthy release. So, before counting any demerits, I now tack on another meditation that's normally separate from this practice called *rejoicing*, in which you review all the good that you've done, to build up a healthy sense of self-worth. I think most of us fail to acknowledge all the good we do in the world and instead ruminate unproductively on our few regrets. To counteract this, in the evening, before bed, you can start by thinking of all the good that you've done that day. Then, after you've felt good about yourself for a while, you can honestly reflect on those words and deeds that you regret. For most of us, they will be primarily verbal, like lashing out in anger or gossiping about someone we dislike. But for some of us there may be physical actions, too, minor or not so minor, like cheating on our taxes or cheating on our partner.

The next step of psychological clearing is to honestly regret those actions in a way that is free from shame and self-loathing. Most harmful actions result from bad habits, and we are now consciously meditating to reinforce more positive ways of being. Without feeling bad about yourself, ask honestly, what would I rather have done in that situation, what words would I rather have said, what actions would I rather have performed? Then, in your imagination, picture yourself doing those things, rehearsing for the next time you're in a similar situation.

After feeling this healthy sense of regret, you then practice a ritualized form of analytical meditation in which you forgive yourself. This step is usually called *purification*, but it feels less religious to call it a *forgiveness meditation*, which is really what it is: you forgive yourself. Like the meditation on impermanence in chapter 6, this self-forgiveness meditation requires no religious belief, though it does involve a form of imagined bright light that clarifies your mind and body.

Because most humans are such visual creatures, visualization can help with psychological healing. At first, I found the whole concept of visualizing myself and my good qualities as light a bit spacey and New Age. But I started to think about generalizing the idea of light to electromagnetic radiation and realized that the powers human beings have to perceive reality, move objects, and sustain life are all based in this ubiquitous energy. Our muscles are electric motors, our cells are powered by electromagnetic fields, and we perceive the outer world through the electromagnetic spectrum.

So, if you find it too religious to visualize yourself as light, just remember that our ability to perceive and affect reality depends almost entirely on the continuum of electromagnetic energy that we are immersed in. It's a thought that's a little geeky, yet wonderfully true.

The last step of this self-forgiveness practice, after the visualization, is to make a resolution not to perform each action you regret for some amount of time. Depending on what it is, you may be able to commit to not doing it for a day, an hour, a minute, or just a second—whatever seems achievable. Typically, you do this meditation right before you go to bed, so a slightly sneaky trick is to commit to not performing a harmful action until you wake up the next morning. The whole process is meant to be gentle on yourself, building up strength through reasonable commitments that are similar to the "One day at a time" motto of Alcoholics Anonymous.

To help remember the process, the names of the four steps all begin with the same letter: rejoicing, regret, remedy, and resolve. These form a four-step meditation on self-forgiveness that is similar to one most Tibetan Buddhist practitioners do at the end of each day. It's a practice that clears your mind (and even helps you sleep better) so you can wake up to be your best self tomorrow. This practice also helps you to take remedial action in the world, like apologizing or otherwise making amends when that's possible. I find this way of ending the day immensely helpful, allowing me to go to bed in a state of peace and wake up the next day with the resolve to be a force for good in the world without guilt, shame, or unrealistic promises that I'll be perfect forever from here on out.

MEDITATION ON CAUSE AND EFFECT

Meditating on cause and effect is a practice of reviewing your actions of the day: rejoicing in the positive and forgiving yourself for anything you regret. It's a process of self-reflection in which you take control of normally unconscious habits that have been conditioned by evolution, society, the media, and your upbringing to steer your mind toward more constructive thoughts and actions.

This practice is usually done in the evening, which helps you process and release whatever happened during your day. But you can also meditate in the morning or some other time and reflect on the past twenty-four hours.

PRELIMINARIES
Settle into a meditation posture, then practice the preliminaries of motivation, refuge, and stabilizing on the breath.

REJOICING
Rejoicing means reflecting on good actions. Think back on your day, from the moment you woke up to the moment you sat down to meditate, and try to catalog all the good that you did. Simply smiling at someone might have made their day. Rejoice in having cooked meals, taken care of your family, or, whatever work you do, having done it well.

Sometimes life gives you the gift of being able to help someone a little more. At the grocery store, if you've ever given someone short on cash a small amount of money, you may have felt their outsized gratitude for your tiny act of generosity. Or you may have felt the appreciation of a homeless person you gave food to after hundreds of people didn't, or a friend's relief after a long walk together when all you did was listen.

For a minute, go through all the good you did today. Rejoice in your good actions and the positive chain of cause and effect arising from those actions that you may never know or see.

REGRET

Now, move on to regret. Regret isn't guilt. Guilt is when you judge yourself and think that you are a bad person for something that you've done. While regret is honestly acknowledging that something you did was harmful to you or to others, sincerely wishing you hadn't done it, and making an effort not to do it again.

Bring to mind one specific action from the day that you regret. Try to see it clearly: what happened, how you felt. This one action can stand in for everything else you regret from the day. Think how much you would have preferred not to have done it. And imagine what you could have done instead: said something different, did something different, or simply not said or done anything at all. Quiet restraint is often the easiest way to avoid doing harm.

REMEDY

Then understand that your actions are part of conscious and unconscious conditioning, the result of the human mind's reactive evolution, imprints made by your parents, your education, your workplace, and the media. Not all your prior conditioning is helpful. You may have been taught that revenge is righteous, rage is empowering, or selfishness brings satisfaction, but such messages aren't in your psychological best interest.

To remedy your regrets, you need to go beyond the rational. Imagine that your body becomes energized and transforms into a hollow shell of light, empty inside. A bright point of light materializes and grows above the crown of your head. That light, like a little sun, is the essence of all that is good and kind, loving, generous, patient, and forgiving. It feels as though the light knows you and everything about you—all your secrets, everything you regret. Yet, basking in it, you still feel loved, accepted, and understood; seen for your true goodness, just like a dear friend would see you.

Then imagine that a luminous liquid pours down into your body from that glowing sphere. It feels warm and cleansing. Visualize your regrets as a darkness that is pressed down by the liquid light, taking on liquid form too, like crude oil, dark and viscous. The purifying liquid light pushes this darkness down, filling your body from top to bottom with clear light, and pressing the darkness out through the bottom of your body. Feel that you are letting go of your disturbing thoughts, words, and actions; you are being forgiven; you won't be bothered by them any longer. The light fills your entire body from head to toe, as the last bits of negativity flow out from you. You are now free from those actions and have completely forgiven yourself.

Rest in the feeling of being filled with light and goodness. Feel renewed. Your goodness is stronger than any of those things that you have regretted and released. Your goodness is your true nature.

RESOLVE

Imagine again what you would rather have done or not done, said or not said, then picture yourself responding in this way. Imagining creates the cause for you to later respond as you would have preferred.

Then make a small resolution not to act in the way you regretted for as reasonable an amount of time as possible—a day, an hour, a minute, or even a second.

If you are going to bed after your meditation, it's easy to resolve to at least not to do it again until you wake up the next morning.

DEDICATION

As you dedicate at the end of this meditation, determine to become more self-aware of the workings of your mind in everyday life. Instead of responding automatically, under the control of preprogrammed habits, try to act mindfully and compassionately, choosing the best course of action—or no action at all. Aspire that your natural response gradually becomes forgiveness, kindness, giving others the benefit of the doubt, showing calm in the face of conflict, and seeing that the vast chain of cause and effect behind everything has little to do with you.

If it's the evening, you can now get into bed, relax, and know that you've made peace with yourself. You might read, watch TV, or go straight to sleep with a clear conscience and a realistic sense of the good that you do in the world, acknowledging the chain of cause and effect that leads us all to do things we sometimes regret.

8

STAGE 4:
WHAT DO YOU DO
WHEN YOU ARE ALONE?

What do you do when you are alone? When you are anxious, in pain, or afraid, when you feel craving or addiction? On the Buddhist path, we call the place we turn to in moments like these our *refuge*. Traditionally, there are three outer forms of refuge where a Buddhist finds solace: the historical Buddha (an enlightened being), the Dharma (his teachings), and the Sangha (his community). A Buddhist's refuge is a lot like the reverence a physicist might feel for Newton and Einstein, the body of scientific knowledge, and the fellowship of living scientists.

Refuge is one of meditation's preliminaries, and in chapter 3's meditation, I introduced a simple refuge practice accessible to non-Buddhists that focuses on humanity's best qualities and your own potential to embody them. Buddhists call this latter aspect an *inner refuge*—a source of strength and support that is accessible to you any time you need it. In chapter 4's nature of mind meditations, you may have glimpsed this deep sense of stability and a capacity for good that is said to lie at the very core of your being.

But refuge isn't only an optimism about your greatest potential. One of the hallmarks of analytical meditation is its clear-eyed view of both ourselves and reality that leads to far deeper happiness than one grounded in uncritical belief. We can be gentle with ourselves and wholly accept our imperfections while still honestly assessing which of our habits bring long-term happiness and which only cause more pain.

We each already have sources of refuge, and some of them may function the way meditation does—helping us to let go of stress, embrace the good in life, and build our character. So we begin this stage of refuge with an honest assessment of what we do when no one is watching.

Refuge in exercise, creativity, and nature

Exercise, art, and music have a lot in common with meditation and are healthy ways to process pain, release stress, and reflect on who you are and who you want to be. Running, playing the guitar, or painting can be rituals for connecting the body and mind, in which you lose track of your worries and plans to become completely engrossed in movement, creation, or nature. I have friends who say their spiritual practice is hiking, yoga, singing, surfing, or sewing. Like anything else, exercise and art can become competitive ego-driven activities. But some of the kindest, most beneficial people I know don't meditate at all and find their connection to the universe—and to themselves—through music, art, or movement. From the Buddhist perspective, it all comes down to your motivation. When activities like these are combined with mindfulness and a compassionate motivation, they become meditations.

Even monks and high lamas use art and exercise as forms of meditation. When I interviewed Dzigar Kongtrul Rinpoche, he told me how his practice of abstract expressionist painting helps him to "not be attached in my creation." And Lama Kunga Rinpoche is an avid golfer who told me that he finds the sport both good exercise and good for developing concentration. *Golf Digest* published a profile on him, "Good Karma Bad Golf," in which Lama Kunga shared delightful gems of wisdom, like "the origins of suffering come from anger, frustration, self-consciousness. If you play golf, you know what I mean."

Work as a refuge

Some of us, when we are alone, find ourselves diving into work. This is the form of refuge I usually turn to when I have an open stretch of time. I'm doing it right now as I write this chapter on a sunny Saturday afternoon. I love pushing the limits of my ability, producing something of value, and growing closer to colleagues who share a common goal. I also like how I lose track of time at work, escaping my worries, cravings, and even my sense of an independent self. There are times when it feels as though I literally become a work of art, a book chapter, or a computer program. I've also found that the intense focus I have while working helps to train the single-pointed concentration required for meditation.

Of course, work can become an addiction or an escape. You can work to the point of burning yourself out, and you can work toward a goal that harms others. "Right livelihood" is a core Buddhist principle from which I have sometimes strayed. Working on projects I didn't believe in felt awful—and made my family feel awful too—because of the painful side effects it had on my mood and behavior.

As long as you aren't doing harm, the Buddhist teachings in relation to work are that nearly anything which makes a positive contribution to the world can be right livelihood. But what transforms work into a character-building practice, or even a meditation, is having a motivation of wanting to improve people's well-being in whatever way you can.

At the start of a meditation session, you aspire to benefit others. But you can do this before you start work too. Motivating yourself explicitly like this may even make you realize that you need to change jobs. This happened to me a few years ago, when I resigned from a company whose practices I found unethical. In Buddhist centers, we motivate ourselves out loud together before a work meeting. "May this meeting benefit others" might sound a little cheesy, but I think that if we had spoken a motivation like that out loud where

I used to work, we would have done a lot more good in the world—and avoided a lot of problems.

Entertainment as a refuge

Entertainment is probably the dominant refuge in our culture today, with our phones a portal to instant diversion. Whether music, video, social media, or the news, entertainment is a way to fill up your mind with external stimulation. Don't get me wrong, I love all these things too. And in chapter 11, I even share a meditation technique called *universalizing*, which transforms any form of pleasure into a profound meditation that opens your heart to others. But when I look at my everyday mind, I don't always have such a pure motivation for seeking refuge in entertainment.

If I'm honest with myself, I mostly turn to entertainment out of habit, picking up my phone when I have a free moment to fill it with something novel, stimulating, or funny. Yet when entertainment is my constant refuge, I deprive myself of the simple joy to be found in the present moment, awakening to what is alive within and around me. There's a Buddhist saying you may have heard that sometimes comes to mind when I reach for my phone: *don't just do something, sit there.*

Sex as a refuge

Another powerful refuge is sex. Based on my own experience with sex—and that of some of my friends—I think this is an important one to discuss openly. When I feel strong sexual desire, I try to become self-aware and explore the space of that experience. Sometimes my sexual desire is entwined with feelings of incompleteness, implanted at an early age by how my parents showed or withheld affection, or by childhood traumas. You can ask yourself whether you are moving toward sex out of feelings of inadequacy, insecurity, or escape.

Sex can be a profound connection with another person, a generous ritual of body and mind. But the routine of sex can also turn into a mindless transaction of satisfying your desire with your partner's body; or even become exploitive sex, where your needs feel so overwhelming that you are willing to use coercion or power, sacrificing another person's well-being to gratify your own cravings.

Pornography has elements of these harms because so many of the pictures and videos online were not created through meaningful connection but out of the actors' desperation and creators' exploitation. I don't think we can ignore the suffering behind the creation of exploitive pornography—and our contribution to perpetuating this suffering when we consume it.

Even with non-exploitive types of pornography made by happy, consenting adults, the recorded act of sex can become disengaged from its purpose of connecting with another human being, instead turning into a lonely activity. A trick of evolution makes us respond to a video's moving patterns of light as though it is a real connection with a living partner. But, like junk food, I find that pornography can leave a psychological residue of dissatisfaction—increasing, rather than satisfying desire. And neuroscientific research shows that addiction to pornography can lead to problems like aggression, poor judgment, and disinhibition.

Substances as a refuge

We all have substances we turn to for refuge. Coffee is one of the most common. Mine are green tea and ice cream. Alcohol, psychedelics, chocolate—none is intrinsically helpful or harmful. Such substances can be used healthily, therapeutically, or in rituals of connection or mind expansion. But it is worth observing your mind as you consume them.

I find the Buddhist approach to eating quite beautiful. It turns a meal into a spiritual practice. There is no universal Buddhist blessing but, before enjoying a meal, you can generate a sense of gratitude for the many people responsible for bringing your food to your plate. You can even think back through the billions of years of evolution that created the diversity of plant and animal life on Earth, realizing that, in fact, it took the whole universe to bring you this meal. "May this food benefit us, so that we may benefit others" is the shortest blessing I know. It skillfully combines interdependence and gratitude, motivating you to eat healthily and be a force for good in the world.

Of course, you can pursue food, drink, and drugs mindlessly, selfishly, or compulsively. They can be huge sources of pleasure and your brain can trick you into thinking that more and more of these substances will bring you ever more delight. But when you test this hypothesis, it doesn't turn out to be true. Overindulging in anything causes the pleasure it brings you to grow weaker and weaker, eventually making you physically ill and psychologically hollow.

When I'm able to wield self-control around substances, I feel good about myself. I like having a choice about what to do in life, and not be dominated by my urges. A Buddhist teacher once shared with me her view that true freedom is the freedom to refrain from desperately chasing your desires, not the freedom to endlessly indulge in them.

Refuge in all beings

Something that often comes to mind when you are alone is other people—whether you are thinking fondly of them, missing them, or resenting them. As Lama Yeshe said, the successful result of practicing the Buddhist path is that your relationships grow stronger. Building deep, warm connections can be our most meaningful accomplishment in life. When I look back on my own life, it is the love, kindness, and respect I have received from others that have helped me most to become a more balanced, present human being. And practically, almost everything of value in life comes from others too—from food, shelter, and safety to knowing how to speak and work.

In Mahayana Buddhism there is an even more expansive way to find refuge in other people than appreciating the direct benefit you receive from them. This greatest source of refuge—even beyond the Buddha and his teachings—is *the entirety of all other beings*, not just those who benefit you. The logic is that without a full complement of friends, enemies, and strangers, not only would there be no one for you to love and care for but there would also be no one's pain to feel compassion for and no one's irritating behavior to stretch your tolerance. In fact, Lama Zopa Rinpoche once complained that everyone treated him too well. With few people to try his patience, he felt deprived of opportunities to further develop this essential virtue.

In a traditional analytical meditation on finding refuge in all beings, you picture everyone you know and feel gratitude toward each one of them for helping you to expand your love, compassion, and kindness. Then you extend this gratitude to all beings on Earth—even those you will never know and those who cause harm—because they help you develop patience, tolerance, and compassion, and because each human being has a fundamental right to a safe, healthy, dignified life.

Who deserves your respect?

In the stages of A Skeptic's Path to Enlightenment, I have purposely left out the topic that traditionally comes at the beginning of the lamrim called *guru devotion*—the unqualified refuge you take in the person who both embodies the Buddhist teachings and explains them to you. Guru devotion was hard for me to absorb when I first began to study Tibetan Buddhism, as I watched everyone around me bow down to Jedi-robed Tibetan lamas and wondered if I should do the same.

We have a healthy view in Western culture that each of us equally deserves life, freedom, and the pursuit of happiness.

But in today's divisive culture, equality also extends to a belief that no one is exempt from our criticism, judgment, and contempt. This makes it hard to look at anyone in a position of authority without skepticism.

Yet, if you are privileged enough ever to encounter someone like the Dalai Lama in person, the experience may prove to you that it is possible to have boundless love and compassion for all humanity and to treat each person you meet like the most important living creature in the world. Meeting someone like this can open up your heart to the idea that some people really are worthy of your unqualified respect. But how do you get to the point of trusting someone that completely? And what if your trust is betrayed?

The lamrim highlights concerns about authority and abuse in its very first topic of guru devotion and recommends that you examine someone carefully for *twelve years* before accepting them as a spiritual teacher. During this trial period, there is a long checklist of qualities you want to observe directly in your teacher, like mental stability, ethical behavior, and compassion, to make sure that this person is worthy of your trust. Those in authority need to walk the walk, not just talk the talk.

When teaching on guru devotion, one of my Buddhist teachers once told us to not only take great care when choosing a spiritual guide but also any potential teacher or boss—even a yoga instructor or a client at work—because we will become more like them. If you think about this for a moment with respect to your current boss, it might scare you. You may even decide that you need to find a new boss, like I have a couple times in my life when I worked for people who behaved unscrupulously. Luckily, the opposite is also true: the nurturing bosses and constructive mentors in your life help you to expand the good qualities in yourself that they embody.

Another important point one of my teachers made is that you don't have to do everything your guru tells you to do. This is critical, because there will always be some people in power—even among Buddhist teachers—who will abuse that power. Reflect carefully on your teacher's instructions but don't let them override your sense of right and wrong, or even what feels healthy or unhealthy, possible or impossible for you right now. Be particularly critical of any advice regarding your bodily integrity.

With these guardrails in place, of examining teachers for years and being critical of their advice, you can then consider the value of respect. This is where it becomes powerful to acknowledge that some people in this world really are more realized and insightful than you or me—possibly even worthy of being bowed down to. This was a hard place for me to get to personally because I was raised by rebellious parents to distrust all authority. However, people like the Dalai Lama, Pope Francis, Anne Frank, Wangari Maathai, or Nelson Mandela really do deserve our respect. And new candidates pop up all the time, like Malala Yousafzai, Greta Thunberg, or MacKenzie Scott. The ones I revere in my personal life are mothers and artists, instructors and inventors and, of course, my Buddhist teachers.

Practically, if there is someone in your life you find worthy of such admiration, it can be useful to visualize them in your refuge practice, as a tangible human embodiment of the qualities you want to expand in yourself, like wisdom, compassion, and mental stability.

The mind as a refuge

After examining all these outer sources of refuge—food, sex, TV, a good book, a glass of wine, a friend, or a personal hero—we now consider our inner refuge, where, within our own mind, we may find an ever-present source of self-respect, comfort, and joy. Thich Nhat Hahn says happiness comes from "a home inside" that you discover through accepting yourself—when you learn to love and heal yourself and are able to create moments of happiness simply by being present and aware.

A good starting point for establishing the inner refuge of your mind is the rejoicing practice, described in chapter 7, taking stock of all the good you do in the world. Next, consider your innate capacity for good, and how kindness and compassion are abundant in societies. Most people live in harmony (despite how it may appear in the news), and living a wholesome, connected life comes naturally to humans, at least when we are free from stress. The Buddhist perspective is that the mind's deepest qualities are ease, openness, and joy. We only stray from our good nature because of bad habits, thoughtlessness, or external conditioning. These habits can be let go by finding healthy refuges.

The fundamental goodness of the mind is an ever-present refuge that requires no elaborate preparation. It is free and always available. As we explored in chapter 4, we can find an inner refuge in the mind's clarity, openness, and capacity for change. By cultivating mindfulness in choosing which thoughts to nurture and which to release, we can effectively steer our mind toward joy, meaning, and purpose, allowing us to become of greatest benefit to both ourselves and others.

MEDITATION ON THE MIND AS AN INNER REFUGE

When faced with fear, pain, or desire, we tend to seek external sources of comfort. This meditation looks at three sources of refuge that are available to us anywhere, anytime: refuge in humanity's best qualities and our own potential to embody them; refuge in those who help us, both through their kindness and in the ways they challenge us; and refuge in the clarity of our inner awareness.

PRELIMINARIES

In your motivation, you can set an intention to meditate to find a healthy, stable foundation of inner support that you can access whenever you need it.

REFUGE IN OUR BEST QUALITIES

Imagine a tiny point of light in front of you at the level of your forehead, like a miniature star, just out of reach. Let the light emanating from that point fill you with all humanity's best qualities—love, compassion, patience, generosity, joy, mental stability, wisdom. If you know anyone who embodies these qualities, you can imagine their mind mixed with the light too.

Now let that point of light float toward you until it rests above your head. Your body dematerializes to become a shell of light. The ball of light, suffused with all those good qualities, melts through the crown of your head and pauses there, spreading white light through your body to make it capable of only doing good.

The light melts down to your throat, where it pauses and turns red, flooding your whole body with its light. Your speech is clarified so that you always know the most beneficial thing to say to the people around you, whether gentle or forceful.

Finally, the light melts down to the center of your chest and becomes blue, again filling your entire body. Imagine that this light clarifies your mind so that you gain complete control over it and steer it only toward good.

Let your heart fill with respect and appreciation for all your own good qualities.

REFUGE IN ALL BEINGS

Expand your appreciation to the good qualities of all the people you love and admire, and those who love and respect you.

Further extend your gratitude to helpful strangers—the people who grow and cook our food, maintain our roads, provide us with safety and security, run our schools and hospitals. Think how the vast majority of humanity spends most of each day benefiting one another in ways both small and large.

Then think of the benefit you gain even from conflicts and challenges. Of course you would flee or seek protection from serious danger, but those people who annoy you and challenge your opinions, whether you agree with them or not, also help you to develop the patience and compassion that are essential to becoming a tolerant, warm-hearted citizen of the human race.

Finally, think about the capacity of everyone to transform and expand their mind as a source of refuge. Each person's mind is subject to change and we all have the capacity to expand our kindness, wisdom, and compassion.

REFUGE IN THE MIND

Now look to the deep source of inner refuge that can be found in your own mind—a healing happiness that comes from simply being present and aware. Instead of denying or rejecting your pain and suffering, totally accept whatever you are experiencing. When you come to accept and understand your own pain, you find a stillness and joy that underlies all mental experience—even loneliness, anxiety, and fear.

Without wishing to change your mind in any way, steer your attention inward. Allow thoughts to appear while maintaining some distance from them. Watch as they arise in your consciousness, take center stage, then fade away. Accept your feelings without judgment. There's no need to push away even fear, loneliness, or pain. Just accept and observe them, while maintaining a stable mind.

As you do this, see that your heart can open. Embrace your thoughts as you might welcome the confessions of a dear friend. See the cause and effect that brings each thought into your consciousness. Feel compassion for yourself as you better understand your desires, pains, and aspirations.

Notice how mental states are impermanent. Your mind has a constant capacity to transform. This flexibility is its natural source of strength. Feelings don't last. They appear, change, and disappear. Even as you hurt the most, those feelings are already fading away.

Maintaining this distance from your thoughts, see that there is an ever-present part of yourself beneath those thoughts, which can't be captured in words. Steer your mind away from coarser thoughts to this deeper, ever-present part of yourself that is clear and unobscured—a part of your mind that allows anything to arise within it without itself being disturbed. Like the scientific view that unobstructed space underlies everything within it, there is an open, unobstructed aspect of your mind at the foundation of all mental experience.

Try for a minute to connect with this deeper part of yourself that is found when you are quiet and alone. It may take more than one session, and it may take more than a minute. Feel free to focus here for longer. The extra time you spend may reward you with experiences you have never had before.

BECOMING YOUR OWN BEST FRIEND

Now you may feel a comfort in being alone, an inner joy— or at least its possibility. You might have felt this at other times—when reading, cooking, listening to music, out for a walk, or absorbed in work. It can be a joy to simply be with yourself, to know yourself at the deepest level. The particular activity isn't what makes you happy, it is merely a pathway to an inner happiness that is always there for you. Meditation can become a reliable route to finding this happiness that comes from connecting with yourself.

Look outward now to the people in your life. See how the joy and comfort you find in them is a reflection of your own capacity to be present and aware, a capacity that is always with you. Some say the greatest gift you can give someone is your attention. And this is the greatest gift you can give yourself as well. The more you meditate like this, the more you realize that you need nothing else to be happy than a little time alone.

The point of meditating on inner refuge is to come to accept yourself and learn to stay with whatever arises in your mind, diving deeper into your psyche to understand who you are beneath your thoughts, feelings, and perceptions. You come to know yourself better, to love yourself, to become your own best friend.

DEDICATION

Emerging from self-reflection, you then find more energy for others. With consistent practice, you are happy when you are alone, and you are happy when you are with others. You are happy when life brings you good news, and you are happy when problems arise. True happiness comes from deep inside, and meditation is a path to consistently find a stable happiness that isn't dependent on people, possessions, substances, sex, entertainment, exercise, or anything outside yourself.

9

STAGE 5:
AM I MORE IMPORTANT THAN EVERYONE ELSE IN THE UNIVERSE?

Robert Thurman once explained the Buddhist view on the root of all human suffering in the clearest, most entertaining way I have ever heard. He said our problem is that, out of everyone we know, out of everyone we have ever met or heard of, out of every person alive on the planet and every other living creature on Earth, each of us believes that we are just a little bit more important than everyone else.

Ask yourself this question for a moment. Do you genuinely feel that other peoples' happiness, goals, and relationships are as important as your own? That their pain and suffering are equally consequential?

Thurman's revelation was so simple—and so funny—that I often come back to it when I feel frustration, anger, craving, or am otherwise caught up in *my* problems, *my* needs, and *my* goals. Of course, in theory, other people's lives must be every bit as valuable as mine. And when I compare the sheer number of others to the singular me, the sum of all their concerns should be more important than my own few dreams and problems. But, for some reason, I find it hard to jump from this logical truth to a heartfelt conviction that everyone else is just as important as me.

Why think about suffering?

The stage covered in this chapter usually goes by the term *suffering*. This was the very first of the Buddha's teachings, now known as the *four noble truths*. Robert Thurman prefers to call these the *four facts*, which I also prefer, because it suggests the empirical, scientific way that the Buddha approached reality, explaining suffering, its causes, and antidotes as experiments you can evaluate in your own life.

Starting with suffering seems like lousy marketing for Buddhism. Most of us don't want to think about suffering at all. However, by understanding our irritation and disappointments, not only do we learn the true causes of our own happiness but we also open our hearts to the suffering of others. Mahayana Buddhism teaches that we can never be happy when we are self-serving. Only through opening our hearts to the suffering of others do we become more loving and satisfied ourselves.

Life is suffering is the traditional translation for the first of the four facts. But "suffering" may not be the best translation for the Sanskrit word *duhkha*. This sounds like a naughty schoolyard word but, in fact, is a complex term encompassing a broad range of concepts. A better translation is "unsatisfactory"—that the ceaseless change we encounter in life is uncomfortable. Problems inevitably arise, and, even in a pleasant life, we still feel unsatisfied despite our increasing accumulation of possessions, achievements, and relationships. Another term people have started to use for suffering is "stress," which captures the ubiquitous type of suffering the Buddha was talking about: everyone has stress, from a homeless person to a billionaire.

There's no way to avoid life's problems, but Buddhism teaches that there are ways to remain happy regardless of what life hands you. I often summarize Buddhism to my friends by telling them that its mind-training techniques don't guarantee that you will be free from problems, only that you can be happy and calm through whatever problems you inevitably face.

Three ways we suffer

The suffering of suffering
The first way we suffer is called the *suffering of suffering*, which sounds like something from that old joke, the Department of Redundancy Department. This encompasses all the experiences that we agree are painful, like poverty, sickness, aging, and death; violence, being criticized, and feeling lonely; the discomforts of heat, cold, and physical pain.

What is the point of meditating on the things that cause us pain? One reason is to become more realistic about anticipating the suffering that we will each inevitably experience. Another is to expand our compassion, recognizing how many other people suffer in similar ways.

Reflecting on suffering also steers us toward healthy sources of refuge to help us cope with suffering, like those we explored in chapter 8—genuine sources of happiness that rely less on the outer world.

But if there were no way to escape suffering, there would be no benefit to dwelling on it. Meditating on suffering would only make us depressed. That's why it's important to work through all four facts, to reach the antidotes to suffering.

The suffering of change
The second type of suffering is the *suffering of change*. This form of suffering better fits the term "unsatisfactory" because it describes the dissatisfaction we feel even as we enjoy the good things in life.

Newcomers are often drawn to Buddhism by this second form of suffering, when they begin to realize that even life's pleasures are unsatisfactory. This is what drove me to Buddhism as I turned thirty and started to check off the goals I had in life—cool job, good reputation, nice place to live, kind partner, shiny possessions—but found that I still often felt dissatisfied, even irritated, for no good reason. Why should that be? The Buddhist answer is that nothing external

114

brings lasting happiness on its own, not even a great job, a beautiful home, money in the bank, or a loving partner.

Some simple Buddhist logic establishes this truth. If external things were the cause of happiness—money, relationships, kids, status—then everyone who had these would be happy. And the more people had, the happier they would be. But as we achieve, consume, and collect more in life, we often become *less* happy, sometimes even yearning for the simpler life we had before.

You can have billions in the bank yet feel unsatisfied. And you can be penniless yet feel content. My father falls into this second camp. He has struggled with money for much of his life, but he is also one of the happiest people I know, delighted simply to wake up each day and bring joy to everyone he sees. Even when I've been angry at my dad, he has remained happy. At the time, I found this exasperating. But from examples like his, we can see that happiness and suffering have mental, not physical, causes.

Of course, there is a basic level of security most people require before they have the luxury of contemplating questions like "What is the cause of happiness?" You may have heard of Maslow's hierarchy of needs—a pyramidal diagram illustrating the different levels of need that people satisfy in turn. At the base are our physiological requirements for food, water, warmth, and rest; then come safety, friends, relationships, and a feeling of accomplishment. Only after securing these do we have time for the luxury of "self-actualization," which includes creative pursuits and a spiritual path.

Feeling jaded, bored, or competitive are displeasures that we still experience at the top of the pyramid of needs because all our wonderful worldly accomplishments aren't fully satisfying. This is Buddhism's suffering of change, which is explained by its three principles.

1. Things change As we reflected in chapter 6, the things we desire change. Objects wear out, delicious foods are consumed, valuables get lost or stolen. We could lose our job or our partner might leave us. We could fall ill or have an accident. And a single social media post could destroy our reputation, whether truthful or not. This is life's uncertainty.

2. **Our mind changes** Even when our treasured objects don't wear out, when we don't lose our job, and when our partner doesn't leave us, our mind can still change. We get sick of our old phone, fall out of love, or grow tired of our job. Just as objects change, our mind, too, is subject to change.

3. **We lose everything at death** The last way of understanding the suffering of change is that even when objects don't wear out, and even when we fail to tire of them, still, when we die, we lose all our possessions and relationships.

Despite its grim observations, contemplating the suffering of change isn't meant to be depressing. The point is to come to a realistic view that external objects can never be wholly satisfying. We need to turn inward for a more reliable source of happiness.

Even though these thoughts reveal the built-in drawbacks of pleasure, the Mahayana Buddhist tradition doesn't demand that you give up life's pleasant experiences. In fact, a surprising side effect of embracing pleasure's impermanence is that, once you do, you may find that you enjoy life's pleasures more fully, appreciating sensual experiences with a lightness and presence that is impossible when your mind is filled with craving.

All-pervasive suffering

The final category of suffering comes back to Robert Thurman's great joke, which isn't a joke at all but the most profound of truths: how each of us inside, deep down, thinks that, out of everyone alive and everyone who has ever existed, we are just a little bit more important. This self-centered attitude, Thurman says—and, of course, the Buddha said first—is that the deepest source of all our suffering is what we usually refer to as *ignorance*—forgetting the interdependence of all beings, placing our own needs above those of others, and failing to care for this planet we all live on together.

Ignorance is the root cause of other types of dissatisfaction. When we counter ignorance with the antidote of wisdom that I share in chapters 13 and 14, we peel away the layers of self-deception to see ourselves non-dualistically, open-mindedly, and generously. Not only do we transcend selfishness but we also transcend "selfness." Seeing reality more clearly, it then becomes possible to find a stable happiness that endures, regardless of our job, relationships, wealth, or status, and whether we are alone or with others.

Buddhism can feel quite academic, with all its numbered lists, but I have found knowing these three types of suffering quite practical. Now when problems arise, I often find myself unsurprised as I remember, "Right, it's that one." And I feel a small sense of accomplishment in labeling my suffering without getting carried away by it.

Just a little more important

The second of the four facts is that *suffering has a cause.* The causes of suffering are dominated by our fundamental misconception that we are just a little bit more important than everyone else, that things must go our way, and that the external universe will bend to our self-centered wishes. We suffer when our fantasy of a world that we expect to always please us is shattered by how the world actually behaves.

It sounds crazy when stated so plainly, but I think a lot of us really do see the world this way. I certainly do from time to time. I expect the universe to only bring me good and for problems to avoid me until I die peacefully after eighty-nine statistically optimal years of healthy life. But we have no such control over the universe; we only have control over our mind. To put it simply, a substantial cause of our suffering is our self-centeredness and the antidote is equanimity—finding a healthy respect for both ourselves and others.

What if I feel less important?

At this point, a reasonable skeptic might object, "I don't feel self-centered at all. In fact, I feel less important than everyone else. But I still suffer."

However, the Buddhist view is that there is just as much ego in feeling inferior as there is in feeling superior. In each, your emphasis is on yourself. When I feel sorry for myself, I'm still thinking of me, but instead of "I'm more important than anyone else," now it's "Poor me."

It's a shame when we feel this way because our lives are profoundly precious. There's so much good we can achieve each day and so much connection we can experience in a lifetime, like we meditated on in chapter 5.

However, if reflecting on suffering still feels oppressive rather than inspiring to you, I want to reiterate that analytical meditations like these are not for everyone at every time. You want to be in a place where you can honestly consider life's drawbacks without falling into despair, and if this meditation doesn't feel appropriate for you right now, it might make sense to come back to it later.

It is possible to be free from suffering

The last two of the four facts are the most hopeful. The first fact is that life is unsatisfactory. The second is that this dissatisfaction has a cause. The third fact is that *suffering can be stopped* or, more precisely, our mental dissatisfaction can be eliminated.

One way to establish this third fact is that you can find people historically, people living today, and even people among your friends and family who don't share the same level of dissatisfaction and who don't get as upset when things fail to go their way. These are the people whose minds are already better aligned with the uncertain nature of reality.

But this third fact, that suffering can be eliminated, isn't necessarily so hopeful either, because, of course, some people are happier and more effective in life than others. This is where the fourth most hopeful fact comes in, which is that *there is a path to eliminate suffering* which anyone can follow.

The fourth fact doesn't magically eliminate the worldly sufferings of sickness, poverty, and death, or even our everyday difficulties. The fourth fact is that there is a path to eliminate the mental suffering that comes from railing against reality as it is, seeing ourselves as more important than others, and expecting everything to go our way. When we eliminate these mental forms of suffering, a natural happiness arises from our mind aligning with how things truly are.

The root cause of suffering is our delusions

Like other Buddhist paradoxes, what the four facts teach us is that expecting problems becomes a source of happiness. Problems inevitably occur. Yet, if we are ready for them, we can maintain a stable, even happy, mind.

This is why Buddhists are always thinking about suffering and death. We're not pessimists. We're realists who want to align our minds with empirically observable inner and outer realities. We call the states of mind that are misaligned with reality *delusions*, and they are the root of all our suffering and dissatisfaction.

If you have experience with Buddhism, you may have heard something different about the cause of suffering—that the root of our problems is not delusions, but karma. In chapter 7, we considered several views of karma, including one Buddhist explanation that karma operates through invisible seeds planted by good and bad deeds from past lives that cause us to find a great job, break our leg, or live a long, peaceful life.

This way of understanding karma can be a huge turn-off for people who can't find scientific evidence for past lives or karmic seeds. And believing in this type of karma can start to make Buddhism seem less like an empirical adventure into the mind and more like another faith-based religion with a set of unverifiable beliefs at its core. Some interpretations of karma can even reinforce social injustice by "blaming the victim" for problems like being poor or getting sick.

A Skeptic's Path to Enlightenment offers a psychological approach to karma in chapter 7, which I call mental cause and effect, but even the traditional Buddhist view of karma isn't as fatalistic as it may seem. It's a common misunderstanding that karma makes bad things randomly happen to you. The teachings on cause and effect—at least in the Tibetan tradition that I'm most familiar with—explain that karma doesn't arise from nowhere but, like everything else, depends on other things. Karma has a cause. Geshe Acharya Thubten Loden describes the cause of karma in my favorite lamrim text, *Meditations on the Path to Enlightenment*: "Just as a seed cannot sprout without the co-operative causes of soil, heat and water, karma cannot ripen without the co-operative cause of the delusions." So, delusions are the main cause of our suffering, not karma.

Diminishing delusions and cultivating positive mental states are what lead to a happy mind. Your future happiness depends on the thoughts you cultivate right now, conditioning your mind to respond either destructively or constructively to future challenges. You can start to reinforce positive mental habits today by cultivating the more realistic view that life's problems inevitably occur. You can't control what happens to you, but you can control how you respond.

The Buddha gave a famous teaching that explained suffering as two arrows flying your way. The first arrow is a difficult event, which you can't dodge. But the second arrow is your reaction to it. You can choose whether that arrow strikes you. For many of us, this second arrow of how we react and ruminate causes us far more pain than the first. This second arrow shot by our delusions is the main cause of our suffering. But the good news from the Buddhist perspective, revealed in the fourth fact of reality, is that we are each capable of reducing—and even eliminating—these delusions.

How to stop our delusions

Our three most powerful delusions are attachment, anger, and ignorance. From a Buddhist perspective, these are the main causes of our suffering and dissatisfaction. Without delusions, we wouldn't suffer emotional distress. If you've been lucky enough to meet people who lack delusions, or whose delusions are greatly reduced, you may have seen this for yourself.

My main motivation for starting on this path was the unbounded compassion, patience, and wisdom that I witnessed in the Dalai Lama. Later, I saw those same qualities up close in other Buddhist teachers—real people who seemed to have eliminated anxiety, compulsive desire, and endless striving. I was able to sit in front of them as they spoke and observe their contentment and joy up close, which gave me real-life evidence for the third fact that suffering can be stopped.

Some of my teachers had experienced far more difficult lives than mine—being imprisoned, tortured for years, seeing friends and family murdered, forced to leave their culture, language, and home. On top of that, they still bore the ordinary sufferings of sickness, pain, financial stress, and the other everyday challenges the rest of us share. Yet I seemed to suffer a lot more than my teachers from much smaller problems with relationships, family, work, and money.

The Buddhist explanation for my greater inner turmoil, despite having experienced lesser outer pain, is that my delusions are the root of my suffering, not my external circumstances. For this reason, the three strongest delusions of attachment, anger, and ignorance are often called the *three poisons*. These delusions poison our ability to be happy, to be present and connected, and to make the most of our fleeting lives. Like other terms we have come across, attachment, anger, and ignorance also have Western definitions, so it's useful to learn the Buddhist ones.

Attachment

The first of our three most powerful delusions is *attachment*. Attachment in Buddhism isn't the healthy attachment psychologists talk about between children and parents or securely committed partners. The delusion of attachment is when you see something you want and exaggerate its ability to satisfy you. Often people translate this delusion as "desire." But there are many healthy desires, like the desire to help others, so "compulsive desire" may be a better term for this painful mental experience.

When you feel attachment, you convince yourself that if you don't obtain that person, thing, or achievement, you can't be happy. This exaggerated view can make you hurt yourself or others to get what you want. You might want sex so much that you are willing to deceive or exploit another person to get it. You might want certain foods so much that you are willing to sacrifice your health and lifespan by overeating. And you might crave money or possessions so much that you are willing to lie, cheat, or steal to obtain them.

The worst part is that, even when you finally get whatever you are attached to, it doesn't bring lasting happiness. That's why Buddhists call getting what you want the suffering of change. External objects lack the ability to fully satisfy us: even a loving partner, a safe home, or a good job. If they did, then everyone who had them would be happy.

I have observed this in myself by paying careful attention to what exactly feels so good when I finally get something that I strongly desire: an achievement, a relationship, a sexual connection, or some financial gain. When I closely observe my mind at these moments, I see that my pleasant feeling doesn't come from obtaining the object; what I actually feel is the more spacious mind of finally being free from the irritation of compulsive desire, at least for a moment.

Giving up attachment

A consistent message of Buddhism is that lasting happiness comes from giving up our attachment. This is something that, to me, feels terrifying. However, I don't believe there's a path to true happiness without letting go of this delusion. I fantasize all the time about what my life would be like without attachment. I especially wonder what I would feel about my wife if I had no attachment. Would our relationship grow even stronger with purely selfless love? Or would our love dissolve without attachment's energy?

I think there is a way to advance gently and patiently toward non-attachment as my teachers encourage. They advise to never get down on ourselves, and to accept exactly who we are each step of the way. Like many of Buddhism's contradictions, acknowledging your attachments—even welcoming them like an annoying friend who you still adore—can have the alchemical effect of lessening them.

The Tibetan Buddhist path can be a little easier for modern people to follow than other forms of Buddhism because it doesn't even require that you give up your objects of attachment. You need to give up your *feelings* of attachment, but you can keep enjoying your partner, your job, your delicious meals, and everything else.

I first learned of this at a Buddhist teaching when one student started scolding another for staying in a fancy hotel. The teacher gently explained that, in fact, a five-star hotel is a perfect place to meditate if you can enjoy it without attachment. He went on to describe the technique of universalizing from chapter 11, that transforms any pleasure into a means for expanding our compassion. I loved hearing my teacher say this because it makes sense. A hotel is a nice place to meditate compared to a chilly mountain cave.

Anger

Anger is the second of our three strongest delusions. Just as attachment exaggerates the happiness an object can bring us, anger exaggerates its harm. I see this exaggeration at work in myself when I get angry at something trivial, like a person sneaking into the line ahead of me. I feel my primitive brain incorrectly interpreting this minor inconvenience as a life-or-death threat. This is a form of projection, the unconscious transfer of our own emotions on to others. In fact, it's not the person who makes me angry but my ego throwing a tantrum when it doesn't get what it wants, however small and petty.

The reality of things that infuriate us is that they have no inherent power to do so. You can prove this by observing how other people feel differently about that same person or action. Politics offers the most striking example, when half the country is enraged by a decision that fills the other half with glee. Your mind gets angry because of its conditioned mental habits, not because of any intrinsically annoying properties of those people or events. Your real enemy is anger itself, not whatever triggers it.

The eighth-century Buddhist philosopher Shantideva offers a thought experiment that demonstrates the absurdity of externalizing our anger. Imagine that a person strikes you with a stick. Do you get angry at the stick? No, you get angry at the person. But if you go slightly deeper, you realize it is anger that drove the person to hit you with the stick, so only the delusion of anger deserves your blame.

There is an important caveat to recognizing the deluded exaggeration of anger. If someone is causing you genuine physical or psychological harm, even though you may be able to let go of your anger toward this person, that does not mean you should remain in the harmful situation. You need to stay safe and, even from the other person's perspective, it isn't compassionate to allow someone to keep abusing you or anyone else.

Ignorance

The last delusion, of *ignorance*, is the root cause of all the others. Ignorance has many forms, including ignorance of the causes of happiness, the causes of suffering, and the interdependent nature of reality. One form of ignorance is rooted in the self-centered view that fails to recognize we are equal to others. To return to what Robert Thurman said, we aren't the most important person in the world, but we also aren't the least important. We each equally deserve happiness and dislike suffering. We are each equally important beings in the universe. Another form of ignorance is even more profound—that our very concept of an independent self is a limiting illusion—which is the subject of chapter 13.

Antidotes to anger and attachment

The antidotes to anger and attachment are similar at this stage of the path: non-reactively watching the mind, accepting impermanence, seeing the faults of anger and attachment, and even seeing the benefits of life's problems. Later, in chapters 11, 12, and 13, we explore the ultimate antidotes of compassion and emptiness. Throught these, we cultivate a boundless love for all humanity and recognize the illusion of an independent self who is capable of feeling angry or attached.

Watching the mind

As you learned in chapter 4, you can productively turn your attention toward your evolving mental experiences of anger or attachment to gain a clearer understanding of these delusions. Notice how your feelings about the object of your anger or attachment are separate from the person or thing that provoked them. Your attachment and anger are not objective realities, but stories you tell yourself from a particular point of view.

It may sound contradictory, but try to watch attachment without attachment, anger without anger. Observe each and notice its exaggerated view. Think of an object you are attached to and see how you exaggerate its ability to please you. Think about someone who angers you and notice your extreme view that there is little or no good to them. Instead of reacting, just watch what is happening inside you. Observe your thoughts and feelings without overly identifying with them, and without letting them take hold of your speech or actions.

Impermanence

Impermanence is another powerful antidote to both attachment and anger. Impermanence helps you see the fleeting nature of everything you desire—and even of desire itself. Impermanence reassures you that feelings of anger will fade, conflicts will calm, and enemies can become strangers, or even friends. At the very least, impermanence tells you that your situation is guaranteed to change.

The faults of anger and attachment

Another antidote to both anger and attachment is to notice the problems they cause. Without anger, you would think more clearly. Without anger, you would have closer relationships, because anger is frightening. You can sometimes scare off a friend, lover, or colleague the very first time you display it. And even if you don't think about its effects on others, free from anger, *you* would feel a lot better because anger is a horrible state of mind to experience. It even causes physical problems like heart disease and high blood pressure.

When I asked Venerable René about anger, he said matter-of-factly, "Anger is the easy one to avoid, isn't it? Because anger doesn't feel good." I nodded as though this was obvious. Then, after our meeting was over, I pulled out my notebook and wrote in huge letters: *ANGER DOESN'T FEEL GOOD.*

When looking at the faults of attachment, you may realize that without attachment you could stop certain self-sabotaging behaviors that hurt your relationships. Without attachment, you might make healthier choices in your life. Eventually, you may realize that your happiness doesn't depend on your objects of attachment at all. You discover a powerful freedom to choose what is most meaningful and beneficial for you and the people around you, rather than being propelled by craving.

The object of your attachment isn't perfect

Another way to counter exaggerated feelings of attachment is to deliberately consider the faults of whatever it is you crave. If it is a relationship you are attached to, you can think how your partner—or potential partner—may initially seem perfect, but almost certainly has just as many delusions as you do, and the two of you would inevitably face conflicts. Buying a new electric car might help the environment and give you a fun ride. But it may also put you in debt, make you annoyed when it gets scratched or stolen, and disappoint you when, finally, it breaks.

You don't think about the faults of attachment to become disgusted with your partner or clean vehicles, but to balance out the delusion that your object is wholly pleasurable and will make your life wonderful forever. When you see the drawbacks of objects that your attachment believes will wholly please you, you are seeing reality as it is rather than through a projected fantasy.

Learning from tragedy

We have all heard of people whose tragedies became turning points of positive transformation: losing a job, getting divorced, even being diagnosed with cancer or suffering the death of a loved one. Calamities can rip us out of a more trivial, unconsidered way of living, forcing us to make changes that eventually make life more meaningful and satisfying. Venerable René had a motorcycle accident in his twenties that made him realize how short and fragile life is. Once he recovered, he began a spiritual journey that gradually transformed him into the skilled teacher he is today, benefiting thousands of students and friends in a way that might never have been possible had he not experienced the shock of his tragedy.

We don't wish problems like car accidents on ourselves or anyone else. And we certainly don't masochistically seek them out. But when it comes to our present difficulties (or ones we resent from the past), it can be healing to think about their potential benefits. It can help us to accept them more easily, work on solutions, and be better prepared for the future challenges we will inevitably face.

I was reminded of the power of difficult experiences by a friend I met up with who had suffered a concussion. In its aftermath, he lost his business and his relationship and was thrown into poverty. I came to lunch ready to offer sympathy and support, but my friend showed up quite cheery. He said his accident had transformed him into a more compassionate, less competitive person that he could not have become without experiencing such a catastrophe. It had also forced him to adopt healthy habits, like yoga, meditation, and lots of time outdoors, that replaced his former unhealthier ways of living.

Gaining control over your mind

Another quote from Shantideva often comes to mind when I am trying to understand suffering and its causes: "If things were brought into being by choice, then since no one wishes to suffer, suffering would not occur to any embodied creature." If each of us truly had control over our mind and understood the causes of suffering and the causes of happiness, then no one would suffer—at least from the mental anguish of our delusions, that second avoidable arrow. Our delusions make life's inevitable problems worse, creating needless additional suffering for ourselves instead of happiness. But, fortunately, there are methods for letting go of the mental roots of suffering and gradually cultivating the true causes of happiness, which you can practice now in this chapter's meditation.

MEDITATION ON LETTING GO
OF SUFFERING

In this meditation on letting go of suffering, you first look honestly at suffering in all its forms. Then you apply antidotes to the causes of suffering—your delusions—to balance out the exaggerated, self-centered views of attachment, anger, and ignorance. The purpose of meditating on suffering isn't to get depressed but to gain a clear-eyed view of reality. You can't avoid life's problems, but if you prepare for them, you suffer less and grow your resilience and compassion.

TYPES OF SUFFERING

The suffering of suffering

The first form of suffering is called the suffering of suffering. Reflect on the billions of people who don't have enough to eat every day, who lack clean water and a safe place to live. Think about the physical pain so many of us feel right now, the suffering of sickness, from colds to cancer; the sufferings of war, imprisonment, and oppression; the natural suffering of aging as our bodies wear out. Think about everyday forms of suffering, like not getting what we want and getting what we don't want; the suffering of loneliness; the instability of our reputation, job, and relationships; the anxiety and competitiveness we feel from life's pressures.

Some suffering we can actively oppose, while other forms are unavoidable. By acknowledging the suffering that we and others experience, we not only expand our compassion but also prepare ourselves better for the problems that we will inevitably face in the future.

The suffering of change

Next, meditate on the suffering of change—experiences we ordinarily call pleasures. Impermanence demands that everything we enjoy wears out or breaks down. Everything that begins also ends—our phones, our cars, our homes, even civilization itself.

But even before things wear out, our minds can change. We tire of the fancy phones we once excitedly unboxed. We grow annoyed with partners we thought would make us happy forever. Our feelings are unstable.

Sometimes our relationships or homes or other durable things do last a lifetime. But then we still must accept that when we die, we will lose these too.

We don't meditate on the necessity of loss to bring us down, but to motivate us to live the most meaningful life possible right now. Realizing everything changes helps us to not sweat the small stuff and to be more present for life's impermanent pleasures and fleeting relationships.

THE SOURCE OF SUFFERING IS OUR DELUSIONS

Now explore the source of suffering—our delusions of attachment, anger, and ignorance.

Attachment: exaggerating the positive

Attachment is when we exaggerate the positive in someone or something; when we look at a product, person, or achievement and all we can think about is how it is going to make us happy.

Bring to mind an object of strong attachment for you. How does your mind see it? Do you believe that if you got it, you'd be truly happy, whether it is some amount of money, someone to love you, or some change in the world? Is this a realistic view? Ask yourself whether your attachment goes beyond healthy goals to become an agitated state of mind that can't be satisfied unless it gets what it wants.

Antidotes to attachment

An antidote to attachment's strong craving is to consider the flaws of the object. Will this person always please you? Will this thing you want work as well as you hope and make you as happy as you imagine? How will you feel if it gets damaged or stolen, puts you into debt, or forces you to work longer and harder? What are the drawbacks of even success, wealth, and fame?

Whatever it is, quietly consider the drawbacks of some object of strong attachment for you. What problems might it lead to in your life? And does your happiness really depend on it?

Anger: exaggerating the negative

Anger is when you see an object, person, or experience and all you can think of is the negative. You exaggerate its power to harm and can't see any good in it at all.

Bring someone to mind who you are angry with—a colleague, a family member, a politician, or businessperson, someone in the world who you feel is harming you or harming others, who you might even consider your enemy. Can you see any good in this person, or does your mind project only harm and annoyance?

Antidotes to anger

Is it possible that many people love and respect the person you are angry with—your enemy's mother, children, colleagues, and friends?

Does this person do good things as well as bad, help as well as harm?

Try to put yourself in the other person's shoes for a moment. Seen from this perspective, do your enemy's actions make sense? Does your enemy feel painful delusions too?

Going deeper, could this person's behavior help you to lessen your own anger by giving you the opportunity to practice its antidotes each day? Could more unbiased insight into your enemy's behavior even help you better oppose the harm this person does in the world?

Ignorance: exaggerating the self
Then look at the delusion of ignorance—ignorance of the true causes of happiness and suffering, ignorance that forgets how things are always changing, ignorance of your interdependent equality with others.

Without judgment, ask yourself honestly whether you think, "I am just a little more important than everyone else—my problems, my suffering, my needs, my relationships?" Or do you feel the opposite, that you are less important than others? Could either of these biased ways of seeing yourself be the root of your suffering? Is it possible to see yourself in a balanced way, not more important or less important than others, but equally deserving of happiness and freedom from suffering?

THE ONLY THING YOU CAN CONTROL IS YOUR MIND
Look at the flaws of anger and attachment. Does getting angry feel good? Each time you get angry, does it increase the chance you will become angry again? When you are patient or forgiving, what habits does that build in your mind?

When you feel attachment, is it energizing or agitating? What habits form when you feel contentment rather than craving?

How much control do you really have over reality, people, and the planet compared to the control you have over your mind? By gaining control over your mind, can you find a more stable source of happiness, and even more stable ground from which to genuinely help others?

GIVE UP ATTACHMENT AND ANGER, NOT PLEASURE OR CONFLICT

Unless your objects of attachment and anger are causing you real harm, letting go of these delusions doesn't require parting from the objects of attachment and anger themselves. When you stop exaggerating the joys of food, sex, entertainment, or relationships, you may enjoy them a lot more, appreciating their impermanent pleasures realistically.

When you let go of anger's exaggeration, do you see more clearly that peoples' actions stem from causes and conditions that began long ago? Can you see how their actions, however misguided, make sense to them? And that a powerful path to resolving conflicts is one of genuine understanding?

Is it even possible to see the benefits of difficult experiences, that they offer you the opportunity to strengthen your patience, kindness, forgiveness, and non-attachment?

DEDICATION

Ending the meditation on letting go of suffering, you can set an intention in daily life to watch your attachment more mindfully, becoming aware of the drawbacks of craving, and choosing healthier ways of responding (or not responding) to your urges.

Also set an intention to notice how your everyday anger may exaggerate the negative aspects of others. Do they do good and kind things too? Are their own minds subject to delusions?

As an aid to remembering suffering and its causes in everyday life, the *four facts*, *three types of suffering*, and *three poisons* are summarized in Table 2.

Table 2: Suffering and its causes

The four facts	
Life is suffering	Nothing external is a lasting source of happiness due to the *three types of suffering*
Suffering has a cause	The cause of suffering is our delusions, especially the *three poisons* of attachment, anger, and ignorance
Suffering can be stopped	Through the ages, wise people have shown that suffering can be stopped by changing our mental attitudes
There is a path to stop suffering	Suffering can be stopped through practices like watching the mind non-reactively, recognizing impermanence, cultivating compassion, and realizing the interdependent nature of reality

The three types of suffering	
Suffering of suffering	Painful experiences like poverty, illness, not getting what we want, and getting what we don't want
Suffering of change	Experiences we normally view as pleasurable but fail to fully satisfy us because they don't last
All-pervasive suffering	Suffering due to selfishness and "selfness," believing we are separate when, in fact, everyone and everything are interdependent

The three poisons	
Attachment	The delusion that exaggerates the positive in a person or thing and makes us want to possess it
Anger	The delusion that exaggerates the negative in a person or thing and makes us want to harm it
Ignorance	The delusion that blinds us to demonstrably true aspects of inner and outer reality, including impermanence, cause and effect, and the ultimate interdependence of all people and things

10

STAGE 6:
THE RED PILL OF RENUNCIATION

There had to be a point in this book where I would bring up *The Matrix*—a classic cyberpunk film famous for exploring the nature of reality and the power of delusions. After meditating on suffering, there comes a profound turning point on the Buddhist path where you decide which direction you want your life to take: toward a continued pursuit of worldly happiness outside yourself or toward an inner source of happiness that relies more on your mind. Metaphorically, you take the red pill or the blue pill—the choice Morpheus offered Neo in *The Matrix*.

For anyone who hasn't seen the movie, its hero, Neo, played by Keanu Reeves, is a small-time hacker who meets a mysterious figure named Morpheus. In the movie's most famous sequence, Morpheus tells Neo that everything about the world he lives in is a lie, a collective delusion that somehow exists only in his mind. Morpheus gives Neo the choice of taking a red pill, that will reveal the true nature of reality, or a blue pill, which will return him to his dreary life. Neo decides to take the red pill. What follows is one of the greatest reveals in the history of cinema, where all that Neo thought was reality turns out to be (spoiler alert) a computer simulation run by robot overlords to enslave humanity.

The choice Neo makes between the red pill and the blue pill is a powerful metaphor for the choice we make to either continue blaming our suffering on external events unwillingly imposed on us, or face up to the true sources of suffering: our delusions of attachment, anger, and ignorance.

Is renunciation for you?

The formal Buddhist name for this red-pill topic is *renunciation*. In the Mahayana Buddhist tradition, renunciation doesn't mean renouncing everyday pleasures or saying goodbye to your friends. Renunciation is something that happens in your mind when you realize that external experiences aren't the true causes of either happiness or suffering.

Of course, the outer world of sense phenomena and experiences contributes to your mental state but, from a Buddhist perspective, the larger factor at play is your mind, not those external phenomena. You can prove this to yourself by observing people's temperaments in everyday life. There are people who have it all, yet are miserable, and people who have many problems, yet remain joyful and at peace.

The idea that happiness comes from your own mind is fundamental to the Buddhist worldview. It doesn't require a belief in the supernatural, but it is a specific point of view. You may find that your view is the opposite, that genuine happiness comes from outside yourself—from a nice life with good friends, family, delicious meals, a beautiful home, comfort, safety, and security. These are all lovely things, and each offers some level of happiness. If you firmly believe that all the wonderful things you experience in the outer world are the sources of a stable, deep sense of happiness, then this next step of Buddhism's mind-focused practice isn't necessarily for you.

I know many people who seem happy with lives centered on family, friends, and the delights of the material world. I told you about my father in chapter 9, who is genuinely happy despite his financial problems. My uncle is also someone I find to be genuinely happy, but who's comfortably well-off. He has a beautiful house. He loves his family, travel, eating out, and has a host of fine possessions. I have most of the same things my uncle has and I enjoy them, too, but I don't think I enjoy them as much as he does. When he and I go out to dinner, I'm particularly impressed by how fully he appreciates a glass of wine, taking every aspect of it all in with vigorous sniffs and swirls.

But I don't believe my uncle is any more of a hedonist than I am. In fact, I'm pretty sure his ability to delight in life's pleasures comes from understanding impermanence a lot better than most of us do, through his life's work helping people traumatized by crimes and disasters survive their experiences. He learned about the fragility of life and relationships by travelling along a different path from my own, and I admire his ability to fully enjoy the moment in ways that sometimes elude me.

In Buddhism, we're encouraged to examine our minds closely to see where exactly happiness comes from. And when you look closely at someone like my uncle, you often find that their happiness comes from something other than their possessions. Wisdom regarding the causes of happiness and suffering isn't reserved for Buddhists, but what Buddhism offers is a precise, proven framework to consistently move us away from our delusions and toward a deeper and deeper happiness that doesn't depend on anything outside ourselves.

Dostoevsky is supposed to have said, "The best way to keep a prisoner from escaping is to make sure he never knows he's in prison." Renunciation is breaking out of the prison of our delusions. It starts with an honest appraisal of our minds right now, which for most of us includes many moments of frustration, anger, impatience, and craving—feelings we'd rather be free from. The red pill of renunciation is the turning point, where we open up to a far richer and more meaningful way to be happy and make the most of our precious lives.

What is renunciation?

Renunciation follows directly from the prior stage of suffering, discussed in chapter 9. *Renunciation* means to give something up. It can sound masochistic, but in the Tibetan Buddhist tradition, renunciation doesn't mean giving up pleasure, sense experiences, relationships, or fun. That may sound like a relief, but giving up suffering requires the courage to dive deep into your mind and face the innermost causes of your suffering.

Some of my Buddhist teachers use different terms for this stage. *The determination to be free* is another way to describe renunciation—determining to break free from the suffering imposed on us by our delusions. The term *self-compassion*, surprisingly, is another synonym for this topic. Self-compassion is not mentioned explicitly in the lamrim, because this idea is so taken for granted in Buddhist cultures, but when I talked to several teachers, they all agreed that the place for self-compassion on the Buddhist path is here in the stage of renunciation. That is because it is in this stage we discover the true, healthy causes of happiness for ourselves.

One of my favorite books is a bulky tome entitled *The Gelug/Kagyu Tradition of Mahamudra* by the Dalai Lama and Dr Alexander Berzin. Across two pages that I have read dozens of times, Berzin writes lucidly about renunciation, describing how, once we reach the stage of renunciation:

> we are willing to sacrifice something. This does not refer to forgoing something trivial, like television or ice cream, or giving up something not at all trivial, like making love with our marriage partner, or even relaxing and having fun. We need to let go of our problems and all levels of their causes.

I often reflect on this as I try to understand renunciation. What I really need to renounce isn't anything material but, rather, my delusions—those self-destructive aspects of my own personality. The self-centered delusions of attachment, anger, and ignorance are what cause us to suffer, which grow into other disturbing mental states like anxiety, addiction, and depression. From the perspective of renunciation, these delusions are what we need to let go of to find true happiness—not relationships, wealth, sex, or ice cream.

You can see how the path takes a turn here, because up to this point the idea of meditation as a kind of treatment for various day-to-day problems makes sense. This is the approach of many popular secular programs and apps that teach mindfulness. Through meditation, they offer an immediate solution to real problems that people experience every day.

Renunciation is the place on the Buddhist path where the rubber meets the road. And it takes serious courage to truly renounce the root causes of your suffering. You have to be ready for this point. And lamrim teachers advise that you may need to meditate for years on the important stages that come before: the precious life, impermanence, cause and effect, refuge, and suffering. Each of these helps you to better understand your mind until you arrive at this crossroads on the path where you decide whether you truly wish to be free from suffering by renouncing its root causes.

Yet renunciation isn't all or nothing. Even small amounts of renunciation can spark great leaps of happiness in your life. To give a small example from early on in my own path, I once asked Venerable René how to deal with the annoying combination of anxiety and ego that I felt whenever I gave a public talk. He told me to pay attention to the Dalai Lama the next time he spoke and notice how His Holiness snapped his fingers as he sat down. This ritual is a reminder of impermanence, symbolizing the briefness of life itself. Rather than thinking of myself before speaking, Venerable René advised me to think instead of impermanence and aspire for my talk to simply be of benefit. I took his advice and almost instantly my anxiety vanished. Ever since then, by coming to an audience with compassion and generosity instead of ego and attachment, public speaking has become a joy.

Wishing to be free from suffering

The basis for renunciation is a sincere wish to be free from suffering and its causes. But understanding suffering isn't like taking a class where you learn the material, pass the test, and move on. Instead, you build up the conviction of wanting to be free from suffering by reflecting on it again and again, like you did in chapter 9. The point is to internalize a deeper understanding of suffering through meditation that eventually changes the way you experience everyday life.

Even highly realized teachers still reflect deeply on suffering every day to keep it fresh in their minds. Lama Zopa Rinpoche's attendant sometimes asked him what he was meditating on. And often Rinpoche said that he was still on the early stages of the lamrim, meditating on the precious life and suffering.

Still, there are other ways to get in touch with the suffering nature of reality besides meditation. Comedians can be very good at it, and the best ones are almost like spiritual teachers in their ability to transform the way we see reality. There was a great Jerry Seinfeld special I saw on Netflix called *23 Hours to Kill* that was all about the suffering of change, the dissatisfaction we feel even with the things we call pleasures. In the show, Seinfeld does this long riff on the suffering everyone in the audience went through just to come to his show. How, when we're at home, all we can talk about is when we're going to leave. When we're on the way there, all we want is to arrive. And, once we get there, all we can talk about is when we need to go home. He climaxes this routine by saying, "Nobody wants to be anywhere. Nobody likes anything. We're cranky, we're irritable, and we're dealing with it by constantly changing locations." I don't think even the Dalai Lama could have given a better explanation of how our attachment can ruin an otherwise pleasurable experience.

Letting go of our problems and their causes

The first form of suffering that we looked at in chapter 9—the suffering of suffering—probably felt straightforward: real-life problems like sickness, aging, not getting what we want, and getting what we don't want. After hearing Seinfeld's joke, the second form of suffering—the suffering of change—also starts to feel more intuitive. Everything we normally call pleasures—the things Seinfeld talks about like going out to dinner, watching TV, and seeing friends—are somehow unsatisfactory to us, too, if we approach them with a craving, dissatisfied mind.

No external thing can please us permanently. Objects wear out and change, as do people and experiences. We exaggerate how much we think we'll like something or someone and then become disappointed when we discover its inevitable flaws. Our mind is fickle and can stop enjoying things we couldn't get enough of the day before. Finally, there is the hovering knowledge that we lose everything at death. The difference between our fantasy and reality can make us anxious and clingy, unable to appreciate life's impermanent pleasures.

Letting go of suffering and dissatisfaction means letting go of their causes: our delusions. At this stage on the path, we need to muster the courage to acknowledge that the sources of our inner turmoil are the delusions that have infected our personality: attachment, anger, and ignorance; and the subsequent ways these manifest as anxiety, worry, jealousy, pride, and other irritating states of mind. You ask yourself, "Do I want to be free? Or do I want to keep going on with a life that feels frustrating and unsatisfactory, that fails to give my ego what it wants, an ego that believes I am just a little bit more important than everyone else in the universe?"

The eight worldly concerns

One of the central ways that Buddhism helps us to renounce the causes of suffering is to enumerate them as the *eight worldly concerns*. These concerns are posed as four sets of opposites that cause us continued dissatisfaction:

- seeking gain and avoiding loss
- seeking pleasure and avoiding pain
- seeking praise and avoiding blame
- seeking fame and avoiding disgrace

When I first heard these I thought, "Huh? What else *is* there?" This list pretty much sums up all of life, at least for me. In some Buddhist traditions, you seek to give up these eight concerns entirely, and live the austere life of a mendicant, which to most of us doesn't sound like much fun. In other traditions, it's a matter of how you engage in these eight worldly concerns—your motivation. This is the approach in Mahayana Buddhism, which teaches that it is possible to engage in the eight worldly concerns if you can somehow do so without aversion or attachment.

Some Buddhist teachers today leapfrog renunciation, skipping to the more captivating teachings about love, compassion, and emptiness. But in the lamrim, those advanced teachings appear last because practicing compassion and emptiness without first realizing the faults of an unexamined life can turn such advanced meditations into biased, selfish activities, like our other worldly concerns.

Lorne Ladner, author of *The Lost Art of Compassion*, once told me that fake compassion is narcissism. To cultivate genuine compassion, you first need to realize the essential truths of life: its preciousness, impermanence, how experience and habits condition your mind, which feelings to embrace and which to let go, and the types and causes of suffering.

You think through the eight worldly concerns honestly to better understand how your own mind and other people's minds work, and whether it is possible to live a life that transcends clinging and aversion. If you came to this book only knowing about mindfulness, you may now be getting a sense of how much more there is to the Buddhist path.

The alternative to renunciation is self-deception

It does seem counterintuitive—at least to those of us raised in Western culture—that the delights of gain, pleasure, praise, and fame, and the discomforts of loss, pain, blame, and disrepute aren't the causes of happiness and suffering. Could Buddhism be wrong in claiming that the delusions of attachment, anger, and ignorance are at the root of our suffering?

I don't think there is a single answer for everyone but, for me, I find that, as *The Matrix* suggests, the alternative is self-deception—telling myself that if I get this one additional thing, I'll finally be happy, whether it is a person, an achievement, some amount of money, or a new possession. There is a character in *The Matrix*, Cypher, who holds this view. He regrets having taken the red pill and wants to go back to The Matrix's simulated pleasures of wine, steak, and sex. Cypher asks the agents to wipe his memory clean so he can return to believing these are reliable sources of happiness. Is that what we want for ourselves?

The stage of renunciation is a lot stronger than the gentle guided meditations many of us start out with to help us sleep better or increase our focus, because now we are looking at the underpinnings of real happiness and meaning in life. Renunciation requires bravery and determination.

Yet, even when we *want* to break out of our self-deception, it can be difficult because we live in bubbles of confirmation bias. On the Internet, we are targeted by information that reinforces a materialistic worldview. Well-meaning friends and colleagues can reinforce our self-deception too. When I think about this, I sometimes remember a story about North Korea's leader Kim Jong Un. Apparently, when he tours one of his cities, workers freshly clean the streets, paint the houses, and fill the store windows with food and products—like stagehands preparing a film set—to make it seem like his country is better off than it truly is.

I have witnessed similar bubbles of denial among the ultra-rich. I had two jobs in which I encountered billionaires—one was Paul Allen, the co-founder of Microsoft, and the other, Mark Zuckerberg, of Facebook. Nearly all the people surrounding these powerful men were well-paid employees who depended on their boss for their livelihoods. I learned that being one of the richest people on Earth can leave you surrounded by sycophants who agree with everything you say, whether or not it's backed up by data—or even common sense. An all-powerful leader paying his staff to tell him only what he wants to hear is a vivid metaphor for the self-denial many of us experience.

The bubble of denial of the powerful and wealthy is also similar to the story of the Buddha's own life. Siddhartha Gautama was an Indian prince before he became enlightened—a boy billionaire like Mark Zuckerberg. The Buddha's parents tried to insulate him from any pain, conflict, or suffering. But there came a point in his twenties when the Buddha wandered into the city surrounding the palace and witnessed for himself sickness, aging, and death—the suffering that we all must face. Seeing the inevitability of suffering made him turn away from his life of pleasure and denial to search for the truth about whatever reality might actually be. The Buddha took the red pill.

The Buddha's view is that renouncing our delusions is courageously renouncing a life of self-deception, diving deep below the surface of our magnificent consciousness to make the most of our precious human life.

Where do we turn once we renounce our delusions?

Where do we turn after we have acknowledged the true causes of our suffering? Chapter 8, on refuge, touched on this, when we discovered that food, relationships, work, sex, money, and friends fail to bring lasting happiness on their own. Refuge and renunciation are closely related, because you can't simply turn away from something, you have to turn toward something too. And there is somewhere else to turn to.

We can realize, through the wisdom of those who have already discovered it for themselves, that we can turn inward to our minds for happiness. We can nurture the noble qualities already present within ourselves by cultivating mental stability, impermanence, cause and effect, and an understanding of the true causes of happiness and suffering. Eventually, in chapter 13, where we explore the final stage of emptiness, we turn toward an ultimate view of reality that completely dissolves the false sense of a self who suffers in the first place.

We can keep learning from Keanu Reeves in relation to this point, as he doesn't only play Buddhists in movies but has also studied Buddhism and supports many Buddhist causes. In a recording he made for the network of Buddhist centers that I am a part of, he explains where renunciation leads us when we realize that external things can't bring lasting satisfaction:

> When we are uncomfortable and anything unpleasant happens, we look to take refuge in something. Usually we turn to food, alcohol, sex, drugs, money, power, or relationships, but none of these things gives us the lasting protection or satisfaction we're looking for. When you understand you can't find lasting happiness, then the desire to find true refuge becomes strong ... To take refuge is to finally seek protection from suffering in a way that can really help you. When we think about the ultimate nature of reality and what causes us to suffer, this is the true refuge.

Renunciation, then, becomes the basis for the most advanced stages that come next on the path: love, compassion, and the ultimate nature of reality. As a bridge to these powerful topics, you can return to the mind as a place of refuge and learn how to gently renounce outer forms of pleasure even as you enjoy them. You shift your focus from what you are experiencing to the process of experience itself. Investigating the relationship between mind and perception in meditation disrupts the solid, external way that things appear. You reveal reality as something more flexible, subtle, and beautiful, an interdependence between mind, matter, and relationships.

The scene from *The Matrix* in which Neo takes the red pill happens only thirty minutes into the movie. And just as there are two more exciting hours to *The Matrix* after this pivotal decision, some of the best parts of the path are something to look forward to for those who have chosen to take renunciation's red pill, which you can do now in this chapter's meditation.

MEDITATION ON RENUNCIATION

Meditating on renunciation means two things: understanding how the causes of suffering lie in your delusions of attachment, anger, and ignorance; then turning away from craving and blaming things outside yourself to find a reliable source of refuge within your own mind.

THE SUFFERING OF SUFFERING AND THE SUFFERING OF CHANGE

First, reflect on life's unmistakable difficulties: pain, poverty, homelessness, sickness, violence, abuse, exploitation, conflict, loneliness, aging, and death.

Think also about how, even when you are free from ordinary suffering, you can still feel dissatisfied with life's pleasures because relationships, objects, and experiences don't last; they wear out, or otherwise come to an end.

Your mind can also change. Recall a time when you stopped enjoying something you had enjoyed only days before—an activity, a person, food, or work—sometimes simply from getting too much of it.

And then remember that you will eventually meet your death and lose everything, a fate none of us can avoid.

DELUSIONS, THE CAUSE OF SUFFERING

Though there is no way to rid yourself of life's difficult experiences, there is a way to be free from the mental side of suffering. See if you can honestly appraise your own mind right now by looking at your delusions. With each, try to understand better how it causes suffering and how its way of seeing is exaggerated.

Attachment

Attachment is a delusion that exaggerates the positive in whatever we desire. Imagine something specific you feel a strong attachment to—a person, thing, or achievement. Is your mind biased in how it sees that person or thing? Do you ignore the drawbacks of what you want?

For a moment, think of all the ways in which your object of attachment is flawed. Is it perfect or does it come with its own problems? Will it truly bring lasting happiness on its own?

Anger

Bring to mind an object of your anger, usually a person. It can be someone from your everyday life or someone famous, like a politician. Notice how anger exaggerates that person's negative qualities, how hard it is to see any good.

Try to recognize that many people love this person— relatives, friends, and admirers. And try to see how this person's actions may benefit many other people too.

Ignorance

Then look at ignorance, the root of the other delusions.

Do you exaggerate your own problems and minimize those of others? Do you believe that you are just a little bit more important than everyone else? What would it be like to see every person as equally deserving of happiness, health, security, and wealth? Though you might logically believe this, try for a moment to truly feel it. Imagine the mental peace that comes from feeling that others are equally important to you, even your enemies.

ARE YOU READY TO LET GO OF SUFFERING?

Consider whether you are ready to let go of the delusions that cause you to suffer. Do you have the courage to admit that external pleasures, relationships, and achievements aren't the ultimate sources of happiness? Is it possible to walk that tightrope of being fully engaged in life without feeling addicted to some people and things, and repulsed by others?

Seeking pleasure, avoiding pain; seeking gain, avoiding loss; seeking praise, avoiding blame; seeking fame, avoiding disgrace. Imagine not running away from these, but renouncing their hold on you. Imagine using life's impermanent pleasures and pains only to deepen your connections to others and do good in the world.

Renunciation doesn't mean that you have to let go of your goals, relationships, possessions, or pleasures. But are you ready to let go of believing that they are the source of your happiness and irritation? Are you ready to commit to an inward journey of discovery to understand how your mind really works and what your mind truly is? Could happiness be as simple as accepting—and then gently letting go—of those troubling aspects of your personality like worry and anxiety to discover a happier, more stable way to live?

THE MIND—YOUR ULTIMATE SOURCE OF HAPPINESS

Is it possible that we each have within us a profound well of warmth, stability, goodness, and satisfaction that doesn't rely on anything outside ourselves? See if you can touch that part of your mind right now. Start by taking a couple of breaths and giving them all your attention.

Now let anything at all appear in your mind. Let thoughts arise and disappear on their own without getting attached to them or annoyed by them. Watch your thoughts from a distance, while letting your mind stay at peace.

Then see if you can explore a subtler level of awareness. When the mind looks beneath thoughts to awareness itself, what does it see? Without any expectations, watch quietly for a moment. You may find that the corners of your mouth tip up into a smile as you find a stable, unending source of happiness deep within yourself.

DEDICATION

To conclude, aspire that any insights you've gained from this meditation might enable you to better understand the delusions that cause your dissatisfaction. Dedicate yourself to seeing the drawbacks and benefits of objects, people, relationships, and experiences more clearly than before. Set an intention to carry the good habits you have built in meditation into your day, so that they change how you see people and experiences—and how you react. Determine to remain in control of your mind so you can choose how to respond to life's urges—following them when they are beneficial or, when they aren't, allowing them to melt back into the open spaciousness of a more subtle mind that is always there for you as a refuge.

11

STAGE 7:
WHAT IS LOVE?

I remember the first time I said "I love you" to someone outside my family. I was sixteen years old and I was in my first "long-term" relationship (all four months of it). I'd been fretting about whether to share my feelings, worried that my girlfriend might not say the same words back to me. If she didn't, I'd be crushed. Finally, walking on the beach, with the drama of waves crashing, seagulls cawing, and a beautiful Californian sunset, I found my chance to say the magic words. And she said them back. Phew.

But what did I even mean when I told her that I loved her? And what did she mean when she said it back? When I once looked up "love" in a dictionary, the definitions just pointed back at one another, describing love as an intense romantic attachment, and romance as a deep feeling of love. A common way we look at love is the quest to find a perfect partner, one who will satisfy our long list of needs and dreams, to whom we will then grant our exclusive affection. But a real-life partner usually falls short of our idealized one, as we share intimacies with a complex human being who has just as many flaws as we do. (My high school sweetheart and I split up the following year.)

Romantic love, and even our love for friends and family, typically comes with strings attached, wanting something back in return, even if it's just love. There's nothing wrong with wanting reciprocal relationships, but it's worth acknowledging the conditions we place on love. Then we can try to imagine going beyond conditional love to the unbiased, expansive form of love know in Buddhism as *loving-kindness*. You can share this more generous form of love with your partner, but also with family, friends, strangers—and even enemies. And though its scope is vast, the Buddhist definition of love is simple: wanting others to be happy.

My mother-in-law was a natural at selfless love, both in her life's work, helping Tibetan refugees settle in America, and in her intimate life with her husband. It came out poignantly in her last words to him as she was dying of cancer, when she expressed her sincere wish that he find another loving partner, so he might happily live out the remainder of his life.

Moments like these make us realize that selfless love is possible in a romantic relationship. But often our love is hopelessly entwined with clinging attachment, which can sour our feelings and make us feel angry, sad, resentful, or afraid when our partner doesn't give us what we want.

The beauty of unbiased love is that it can be conjured systematically, whether you're in a relationship or not, and even when you are alone. One way is to imagine the people close to you and offer them whatever they need to be happy. You gradually expand this selfless love to people who are more distant, including strangers and enemies. The result of cultivating love in meditation is that eventually you are able to offer your love freely to everyone you encounter in everyday life.

Of course, there is no guarantee that life's myriad causes and conditions will allow you to make other people genuinely happy, even if you give them everything they want. But in another of Buddhism's ironies, by meditating on loving others, you yourself become happier.

What is compassion?

Like Buddhism's uncomplicated definition of love as wanting others to be happy, its definition of compassion is equally simple: wishing to take away others' suffering. Compassion is different from empathy, which is feeling someone else's pain. Compassion starts with empathy, but goes beyond it by wanting to do something about it—in real life, if possible but, at the very least, in your mind.

There is a condition called "compassion fatigue" that nurses, doctors, and therapists sometimes suffer. But if we are using the Buddhist definition of compassion, we should more precisely call this "empathy fatigue." Empathy can make you feel overwhelmed by someone else's suffering, wanting to flee their pain. But compassion gives you the energy to engage with a person's suffering and work to lessen it. Robert Thurman says compassion is empathy plus courage.

Cultivating compassion in your meditation is similar to cultivating loving-kindness. One way to start is by imagining the suffering of someone you love and wishing to take it away. Then you gradually expand your compassion to family, friends, acquaintances, strangers, and, eventually, even your enemies, wishing to take away their pain too.

Selfish altruism

In Mahayana Buddhism, love and compassion are inseparable from altruism, giving without expecting anything in return. There is even a special word for the altruistic wish to give all beings everything they need and eliminate all their suffering: *bodhicitta*, which means the "mind of enlightenment." The fact that the very word for enlightenment, *bodhi*, is synonymous with compassion shows how fundamental altruism is to Mahayana Buddhism.

Altruism isn't a religious requirement for being a Buddhist. Rather, it is seen as the inevitable outcome of realizing the equality of all human beings' needs: that everyone wants to be happy and no one wants to suffer. With its logical arguments for unselfishness, Mahayana Buddhism is related to Western philosophies like utilitarianism and stoicism, which propose doing good as a rational response to analyzing the human condition.

The other argument in Buddhism for altruism is that thinking and acting from a base of love and compassion is the way to be happiest yourself. The Dalai Lama talks about this all the time. In fact, these were the first lines I highlighted in the first book of his that I read:

> If you would like to be selfish, you should do it in a very intelligent way. The stupid way to be selfish is seeking happiness for ourselves alone. The intelligent way to be selfish is to work for the welfare of others.

Of course, you don't have to be a Buddhist to be an altruist. One extraordinary example is James Harrison, who has donated his rare blood type every few weeks for 60 years to save the lives of nearly 2.4 million babies. Another story that has stuck with me is that of Zell Kravinsky, who first gave away his 45-million-dollar fortune. Then, still not satisfied (and despite his family's objections), he gave away one of his kidneys to save a stranger's life. Examining their lives of privilege rationally, these people decided altruism was the logical way to live a happy, meaningful life.

Buddhist teachings makes it clear, however, that no heroic acts are required to live an altruistic life, and that it is also critical to take good care of yourself. But when does healthy self-care turn into the unintelligent form of selfishness that the Dalai Lama talks about? One of my teachers says it arises with the thought of me and mine: *my* coffee, *my* car, *my* phone, *my* lunch, *my* job, *my* friend, *my* partner, *my* happiness; the idea that as long as I get mine, I'm okay.

It's a common view today that if we all act selfishly and simply avoid harming one another, we will create a happy world where everyone takes care of themselves. This is the philosophical view of *egoism*. But we have nearly perfected this self-centered philosophy in the United States, and has it created a happy country?

The Buddhist view is that the path to happiness is the reverse of this. It is thinking of you: *your* happiness, *your* welfare, *your* partner, *your* coffee. This is being intelligently selfish. Another way the Dalai Lama puts it is, "If you want to be happy, cherish others."

Tasting the chocolate

Venerable René says that talking about love is a lot like talking about chocolate. You can talk about it as much as you like, but to truly experience it, you have to taste it. You probably remember the first time you were pierced by romantic love, like me and my high school sweetheart—an extraordinary experience that transcends any description you've ever read, heard, or seen. And it's the same with the selfless love of loving-kindness.

You may have a parent who has shown you unselfish love from an early age or a generous friend who is always there for you whenever you're most in need. But, for me, the greatest selfless love I have experienced has come from my Buddhist teachers, who emanate boundless affection for each person they encounter.

This chapter includes four meditations to cultivate such open-hearted states: love, compassion, equanimity, and a lesser-known practice called *universalizing*, which transforms everyday pleasure and pain into boundless love and compassion.

It can take some effort to kindle such expansive forms of love and compassion when you start from a more self-centered state (it certainly does for me). But I've found that once you feel even a spark of loving-kindness or compassion, it becomes easier to sustain and grow it through repeated meditation.

MEDITATION ON LOVE

LOVING YOURSELF

Start by imagining yourself where you are, with your mind at peace. At your heart is a glowing orb filled with all your best qualities: kindness, openness, generosity, patience, humor, resilience, joy.

Now imagine another copy of you across from yourself, alive and at peace. See this other you as you would a dear friend. Think of all your good qualities, all the good that you do in the world, the positive impact you have on your friends, family, work, and the causes you believe in.

Think also of the ways you sometimes hurt others or hurt yourself due to confusion, mistakes, or wounds— rarely on purpose but due to the many causes and conditions that have shaped your life.

Send love to the you across from you on a beam of light that connects your hearts. Through it, wish yourself good, offer yourself whatever you need materially, and also whatever love, friendship, and support you need too.

LOVE FOR A LOVED ONE

Let the you in front of you dissolve away. Then, in the same spot, materialize someone you love dearly and easily. For some, a child or friend might be easier than a partner or parent.

How does your love make you feel? Does your genuine affection crowd out more anxious, self-absorbed thoughts?

Imagine how the other person feels being loved, virtues appreciated, faults accepted, mistakes forgiven.

Feel your love and this person's gratitude for being loved exchanging between you on a beam of light that connects your hearts: love, inexhaustible, made visible in your mind.

LOVE FOR PEOPLE CLOSE TO YOU

Now let people close to you appear beside and behind the person you love. Let your feelings of love—as light from your heart—spread to each of them on individual beams and rest in your love for all of them.

LOVE FOR STRANGERS

Next, imagine a vast crowd of strangers surrounding you and your loved ones, the billions of people on Earth. Visualize billions of individual light rays going out from your heart to theirs, giving them everything they need—wealth, safety, friends, and affection.

LOVE FOR ENEMIES

Finally, imagine the people you have difficulty with appearing in front of you. These are people who have hurt you or caused pain to those you care about. Do they also fundamentally want to be happy? Do they want to be loved too? Perhaps if they were genuinely loved, they would stop creating problems for you and for everyone else.

If you can, imagine offering your enemies happiness and its causes—the material things they need, security, friends, mental stability, and a warm heart.

DEDICATION: BRINGING LOVE INTO EVERYDAY LIFE

Let this huge crowd of people and the light rays of your loving-kindness dissolve into diffuse white light. Let your body return to awareness of itself and the room around you. As you open your eyes, see if you can maintain the expansive feeling of wishing all beings happiness. Take a deep breath in, let a deep breath out, and aspire to carry this inclusive feeling of kindness and affection into the rest of your day.

MEDITATION ON COMPASSION

SELF-COMPASSION

Imagine a copy of yourself seated before you—alive, at peace. Try to see yourself as you would your best friend, as kind, loving, patient, wise, joyful, and generous.

When you don't act from these aspects of your deepest nature, could these merely be temporary delusions, unhelpful habits that you can let go?

Think of the problems you have with your body, job, money, or relationships; think of your internal challenges with anger, craving, selfishness, jealousy, or pride. It's natural to have difficulties, and it's natural to have habits that you want to change. Good things happen slowly, both outside and within.

Feel compassion for yourself, wanting to take away all your pain. Then imagine doing so in real life—eliminating physical, financial, family, and relationship problems; leaving you only with the health, safety, wealth, and love that you deserve. Imagine that your mental problems fade away, too, into the abundance of both your inner goodness and all the good that you do in the world.

COMPASSION FOR A LOVED ONE

Now dissolve the other you and materialize in that place someone close to you who is facing challenges. What problems does this person have and how do they feel about them?

Sincerely wish to take those problems away.

Then imagine that you have succeeded. How does your friend feel, free from all those inner and outer obstacles, living in perfect health, wealth, safety, and mental peace?

COMPASSION FOR ALL BEINGS

Extend your compassion to people you know and care about who face challenges—even huge obstacles like illness, money, the environment, inequity, or injustice. How wonderful would it be if they could be free from their problems? With whatever ability you have, determine to help take those problems away. And imagine for a moment that all their problems vanish.

Consider all other forms of suffering on Earth for all other human beings, even those you don't get along with or despise. Can you empathize with their suffering, too, even wish to take it away? Imagine that all their suffering has actually been taken away.

DEDICATION: TAKING COMPASSION INTO DAILY LIFE

Even though you can't solve everyone's problems through meditation (or any other means), this attitude of at least wanting to take away their problems is a powerful tool to make your life as meaningful, happy, and beneficial as it can possibly be. Try to take this mindset into your day, directing your energies outward with compassion and the wish to alleviate others' suffering.

Equanimity

When I was in my twenties, my father got married a second time. After the ceremony, he had all the guests line up in two concentric circles to walk in opposite directions and say to one another, "I love you." For some reason, this ritual really annoyed me. I didn't want to tell strangers that I loved them. That feeling was supposed to be hard-earned and exclusive.

I snuck away before the whole thing was over, finding it almost unbearable to offer such intimacy to strangers.

You may have found the last stage of the meditations on love and compassion as difficult to practice as I found saying "I love you" to those hundred people at my dad's wedding. This is normal. Even in your imagination, it can feel hard to extend love to strangers, and downright painful showing kindness to those who have hurt you or who hurt the world.

Of course, if you have been seriously harmed by acts of violence or trauma, you may not be ready to bring those people into your meditation at all. Meditations on love and compassion are considered advanced practices. That is why you find them here at the end of the path. However, there is a way to build up to love and compassion more gradually, by first meditating on the foundational practice of *equanimity*.

In everyday life, most of us are torn between attachment to our loved ones, anger at those who give us trouble, and apathy toward people we don't know. But the Buddhist perspective— and, hopefully, common sense—is that all people deserve to enjoy happiness and avoid suffering.

Equanimity is a technique for developing these healthy feelings of connection to others—even those you despise. You don't hear as much about equanimity as you do about mindfulness, love, and compassion, but in the Tibetan Buddhist tradition, equanimity is an essential step you take *before* love or compassion. That's because without equanimity, your mind remains biased in its feelings toward others, and true compassion is impossible.

When I first heard the logic of equanimity, compassion, and loving-kindness, the arguments all made sense intellectually. But I still found expanding my affection beyond my loved ones threatening, because I worried that I would lose the special feelings I had for the people closest to me. Yet I soon learned that none of these techniques tells you to reduce the love you have for those dearest to you. Even the Dalai Lama has best friends. Instead, equanimity expands your capacity to care so that the closeness you now reserve for just a few gradually opens up to acquaintances, strangers, and even enemies.

"Loving" a stranger doesn't mean letting down all your boundaries or trusting them uncritically. And loving an enemy doesn't mean you won't stop fighting the harm that person causes in the world. Loving an enemy may not even entail ever speaking to or coming near that person again. Loving-kindness is a mental attitude that benefits you more than anyone else, by seeing that there is good in everyone, even as you remain critical and engaged in defending what you believe is right in the world.

As you decide whether to open your heart up to your enemies, it can be helpful to first think, selfishly, whether it feels good to be angry at them. Is this a state of mind that you want to be free of? Or does anger motivate you to do important good in the world? I've heard people ask the Dalai Lama whether the galvanizing power of anger is, in fact, critical to fighting injustice, but he has always answered similarly by acknowledging that yes, anger *is* motivating, but it's like taking a powerful drug. Anger gives you energy, but it has negative side effects that, in the long-term, hurt your well-being.

The motivating power of anger can quickly spiral out of control, clouding your good judgment and making you feel terrible and even do terrible things. The persistent anger that you hold toward enemies can spill out to break up your good relationships with friends and family. And researchers have found that the stress of habitual anger can lead to physical illness and even death.

What the Dalai Lama has also said, though, is that there is an equally motivating emotion which has none of anger's negative side-effects. That emotion is compassion. And the first step toward compassion is equanimity, in which you simply equalize your feelings toward others without trying to be an altruistic saint.

I was deeply moved by Tara Brach's explanation of a gentle path we can take to gradually let go of any anger that blocks us from equanimity. She says that a period of anger is often necessary to energize and armor ourselves, especially if we've been abused or traumatized. Thinking we must immediately forgive someone who has hurt us only piles shame on top of our anger. But, overall, anger is just an early, powerful signal of something even deeper that underlies it. And, at some point, we need to connect with what that is.

Equanimity is for that moment when your initial flare of energizing, armoring anger has dissipated and you dive courageously beneath your surface feelings, beyond a view centered on yourself, to take in the bigger picture. When you are ready to move past anger, you reap massive rewards, enlarging your feelings of connection with everyone, even your enemies.

Friend, enemy, or stranger?

The first step in the practice of equanimity is to notice how we instinctually categorize people into friend, enemy, or stranger based on how they treat us. These are biased labels based on their transient relationships to us. There's nothing wrong with labeling people as "friend," "enemy," or "stranger," but being more precise about what these terms mean is the first step toward cultivating equanimity.

Friends are people who help us. We feel happy when we see them and go out of our way to help them. They seem to only want our happiness. And, in return, we only want them to be happy too. Friendship can extend to people we don't know personally, like the heroes we admire who care for others, improve society, or protect our planet.

Enemies are people who harm us. They go against our wishes. They say things that displease us. They may do this because they have different beliefs and values from ours. Or they may harm us for more personal reasons, motivated by conflict, resentment, jealousy, or revenge.

We each also have broader enemies in the world— politicians whose policies we abhor, mass shooters who kill innocent children, corporate leaders who harm society or the environment—anyone opposing what we think is just. Each of us can name specific people in the world doing what we believe is drastic harm to certain racial or ethnic groups, women, refugees, our country, or the environment.

Strangers are people who don't appear to harm or help us: assistants in stores, the person beside us on the bus, workers repairing the road. As they don't appear to have either a direct positive or negative impact on our life, we tend to feel indifferent toward them. We hardly notice them, and we are generally unconcerned about their welfare. Robert Thurman uses the term *numbness* to describe the feeling we often have toward strangers—an everyday sense of disconnection.

In Buddhism, the view is that our biased way of feeling differently about friends, enemies, and strangers is at odds with reality. Labels like "friend," "enemy," and "stranger" are only based on how people momentarily help us, harm us, or are of no concern to us.

Relationships change

Not only is our view of who is a friend, enemy, or stranger biased by short-term self-interest but these relationships also change. In the equanimity meditation, we recall that people can shift between being our friend, enemy, or stranger.

It's easy to see that every friend or enemy you have was once a stranger. And each of us has friends who have drifted away to become people we rarely think about. Friends can become enemies, too, sometimes over a single harsh sentence or a romantic rivalry. In fact, romantic relationships are the most dramatic examples of how we cycle through all three of these categories. I am happily married now, but I was married once before. I remember opening my front door to the woman who became my first wife thinking, "Who is this incredible person?" and hoping we might quickly become non-strangers. Then I remember, years later, as we were yelling at each other in one of our final arguments, feeling that we had become each other's worst enemy. A dozen years later, I came across my ex-wife at a company where we were both working. By then she had again become a stranger, who I had stumbled upon, giving a great talk. Reacquainting ourselves over tea afterwards, we once again became friends, falling into comfortable jokes and confessions, our anger and resentments forgotten.

The transformation from enemies to friends is rarer, but it does happen. One of my favorite examples is the story of Black civil rights activist Ann Atwater and C. P. Ellis, the "Grand Exalted Cyclops" of Durham, North Carolina's Ku Klux Klan chapter. In 1971, the courts ordered the city to desegregate its schools and appointed these two enemies to lead ten days of grueling meetings to arrive at recommendations for the school board. Despite Ellis arriving at their first meeting with an automatic weapon, miraculously, he and Atwater become friends through the process, uniting against economic disparities that affected both white and Black children in their community. On the final day of the meetings, Ellis tore up his Klan card, to become a lifelong advocate for civil rights and a cross-racial union organizer. He and Atwater remained friends for the rest of their lives. And when Ellis died in 2005, Atwater gave the eulogy at his funeral.

Transforming bias with equanimity

If a Klan member and a Black civil rights activist can transform their bias, then there is hope that we can too. Meditating on equanimity gives us a structured technique to pull ourselves out of our one-sided views and into the minds of others. Through the power of imagination and empathy, the logic of equanimity has us contemplate three points:

1. **other people see our friends, enemies, and strangers differently** our point of view is only one of many

2. **relationships change** friends, enemies, and strangers can quickly switch categories as we face conflicts and share joys

3. each of us wants to be happy and doesn't want to suffer
whether friend, enemy, or stranger, our rights and needs are
fundamentally the same.

Though meditating on equanimity can be powerful, equanimity
isn't a "law of attraction" that says visualizing your enemy
changing into a friend will make you best buddies. The point is
to bring your own mind into alignment with the ever-changing
nature of reality and to realize that your hard views of who
is an enemy, friend, or stranger are inaccurate. In truth, all
relationships are fluid.

Keeping your mind free from anger toward enemies and
biased attachment toward loved ones makes you more effective
at taking care of others, and even at changing the world.
Consider people who have mastered equanimity, like the Dalai
Lama. If you've ever come face-to-face with him—or someone
like him—the equal affection he offers everyone he encounters
is palpable, yet disconcerting.

A friend of mine once had a chance to offer the Dalai Lama
a gift at the beginning of public teachings. He chose to offer
one of those roll-up Tibetan paintings of Buddhas you may
have seen called a thangka. As my friend handed His Holiness
the expensive work of art, he said that he felt the most
profound sense of being loved, fully known down to his core,
accepted even for his faults. He was thrilled to offer this fine
present to his teacher.

Then, in the afterglow backstage, the person who had
been in line behind my friend walked up and said, "Look
at this beautiful thangka the Dalai Lama just gave me!" In
an act of non-attached generosity, the Dalai Lama had
immediately passed my friend's gift on to the next person in
line. My friend admitted to me that he actually felt jealous,
disappointed that the Dalai Lama's affection wasn't biased
toward him.

I appreciated my friend's honesty in sharing his story,
because I've had similar thoughts with great teachers, feeling

disconcerted at the equal love and attention they offer
everyone. It's a little painful to admit that I am biased even
with my spiritual teachers, wanting them to treat me as though
I were more special than other equally deserving students.
But such feelings have also given me one more opportunity to
meditate on equanimity, working through the attachment I
feel even to my teachers.

Equanimity as universal human right

Meditating on equanimity offers you a powerful exercise
in non-discrimination, filling your mind with genuine
understanding of how relationships are impermanent. Your
enemy could become a friend. Your friend could become
a stranger. And each stranger has the potential to become
the dearest person to you on Earth. Its structured analytical
meditation gradually fills you with respect for all beings, based
both on the impermanent nature of relationships and our
universal human rights: we all want to be happy, none of us
wants to suffer, and achieving happiness for everyone—even
our enemies—would make the world a better place.

It's worth thinking about how unjust the world remains
because it lacks a grounding in equanimity. Kim Stanley
Robinson has written that, until we treat all beings equally
and we all have the same opportunities for health, happiness,
and security, "we remain stuck in some kind of prehistory,
unworthy of humanity's great spirit." This is a powerful,
humbling idea: that humanity hasn't yet begun until everyone
enjoys their equal rights and protections.

Treating others equally starts with each of us not only
recognizing everyone's universal human rights intellectually
but also feeling this to our very core. This Buddhist approach
to meditating on equanimity is a path to get there. At first,
meditating on equanimity takes work. But, eventually,
equanimity becomes something you feel instinctually whenever
you see, or even think about, another human being.

EQUANIMITY MEDITATION

Before starting a painting, an artist primes the canvas so that it takes all colors equally. This meditation does the same for your mind, diminishing your bias so that you equally respect all beings.

FRIEND, ENEMY, AND STRANGER

Start by imagining that there are three places for people to sit in front of you.

On the left, picture a friend. Let your natural affection for that person fill you. Notice how you want your friend to be happy—and how happy your friend makes you. Also notice how you have a strong, clear belief that this person is *my* friend, almost as though this has always been so.

In the middle, picture an enemy—someone who is unkind to you, who makes you angry, who doesn't give you what you want. If you have an actual enemy in your life, picture that person. If not, choose someone you perceive as an enemy to kindness, equality, or to others' happiness. This could be a political leader, a violent criminal, or a corrupt CEO, someone who harms the planet, or someone who holds racist or sexist views. Once you have chosen a specific person, materialize this enemy sitting before you.

Examine this person who hurts you, who hurts others, who makes you angry. Allow your negative feelings to arise, but then let them pass through you, observing them without judgment.

Now, on the right, materialize a stranger. Choose someone specific. It could be someone you passed on the street today, someone you bought your coffee from, or someone who drove by in a car. Try to remember the person's face, body, and clothing as you visualize this person on the third seat in front of you.

How much do you care for this stranger? How much are you even aware of this person's presence? Offering little benefit or harm to you, this stranger may seem of no importance to your life.

Step back and see how your feelings for these three people are based on what each of them does or doesn't do for you, and how their roles in your life seem fixed as a friend, enemy, or stranger.

But are these relationships as stable as they seem?

ARE FRIENDS STABLE?

Bring your attention to your friend on the left. Have you ever had a friendship that ended—maybe over a few words? Can you imagine one sentence your friend could say that would make you consider your friend an enemy? What if your friend said, "I hate you," or criticized you, or declared allegiance to a different political party?

Your close friends know everything that you are most sensitive about, so they could hurt you deeply if they wanted to. What would happen if the friend in front of you hurt you like that? How would your feelings change? Quickly or gradually, would you shift from seeing this person as a friend?

CAN ENEMIES CHANGE?

Now bring your focus to your enemy, sitting in the middle. Have you ever had an enemy who became a friend? Do you remember how it happened? Was it something the person said or did, even something small? Or did you come together through some common purpose?

Imagine what could bring you together. For a co-worker, perhaps teaming up for an important project that you couldn't do alone. With a belligerent neighbor, imagine a disaster uniting you to protect each other like friends. Or for estranged friends or family, imagine them—or you— falling gravely ill, and putting your conflict into perspective. If your enemy said just one kind word about you, how might your heart soften?

If your enemy is more distant, like a political leader, what could this person do to make you let go of your hatred? Apologize, resign? What if your enemy renounced all the positions you disagree with and took up the causes you believe in? However unlikely, imagine this happening in real life and see how your feelings might change, even toward a person you totally oppose.

STRANGERS BECOME FRIENDS OR ENEMIES

Now think about the stranger on the right. Imagine the person performing one act of kindness. It could be as simple as a barista giving you a free coffee. You might then learn this stranger's name and start telling people, "I have a friend at the café."

Or imagine the opposite happening: with a single dirty look, you might start to consider this person your enemy. You might even boycott the café.

Try to remember how you felt about other people you now consider friends or enemies. Can you remember how they seemed to you when they were strangers?

Draw back to see all three people clearly again. How much more fragile and changeable are these relationships than you initially thought? Is this a disappointment, a relief, or a revelation? Is anyone permanently a friend, enemy, or stranger?

HOW OTHERS SEE OUR FRIENDS, ENEMIES, AND STRANGERS

Now look at the three people from outside your own point of view.

The enemy and stranger probably both have people who love them more than anyone else in the world. They may have a caring mother and father, a partner devoted to them, children who look up to them and rely on them for their survival.

Think how your dear friend has enemies: ex-lovers, competitive colleagues, or broader, vaguer enemies—people who hate your friend for specific beliefs or lifestyle choices, just as each of us may dislike some groups of people for holding views that we don't agree with.

HOW FRIENDS, ENEMIES, AND STRANGERS SEE THEMSELVES

How do your friend, enemy, and stranger see themselves? Do they each want to be happy just as much as you do? Do they each equally dislike suffering? Do they each deserve the same rights and have the same needs as everyone else?

DEDICATION: EQUANIMITY IN EVERYDAY LIFE

As you come out of this meditation, examine what equanimity does to your state of mind. How might it change the way you engage with the world? Could you remind yourself of the equality between friends, enemies, and strangers as you encounter people through the rest of your day?

Going beyond yourself

The final meditation in this chapter is one of the most powerful antidotes that I know to the self-centered delusions of attachment and aversion. It uses love and compassion to counteract every single instance of craving or annoyance that we have, right as we experience them. This technique, called *universalizing*, transforms both our problems and our joys into ways of opening our hearts to others.

Earlier in this chapter, I mentioned bodhicitta—the altruistic wish to attain enlightenment for the benefit of all beings. This view is the total opposite of self-centeredness. In Buddhism, a being who commits to this ideal is called a *bodhisattva*. Some Buddhists embrace this ideal so fully that they take a vow to pursue it for the rest of their lives (and, for those who believe in them, for all their future lives too).

As it is almost impossible to uphold, people who take the *bodhisattva vow* generally renew it every day. The Dalai Lama himself does this each morning with these awe-inspiring verses from Shantideva's poetic treatise on compassion, *A Guide to the Bodhisattva's Way of Life*:

> For as long as space remains
> For as long as sentient beings remain,
> Until then shall I too remain
> To dispel the miseries of the world.

It might seem that such a heroic attitude is only suitable for saints and altruists like the Dalai Lama, Gandhi, Desmond Tutu, or the benevolent physicians of Doctors Without Borders. Yet bodhisattvas also face problems and experience pleasures. What do they do with these feelings? Instead of fleeing pain and pleasure like an ascetic, they use everyday pleasure and pain as fuel to move them toward more enlightened ways of being.

Universalizing

Universalizing is both simple and profound. The idea is to apply a universal antidote to the attachment and aversion that we feel when we experience pleasure or pain. We do this by bringing others to mind and, in our imagination, sharing our pleasure with them or wishing to take away their pain.

Often, when we experience a setback, our mind tightens into itself, feeling angry, jealous, betrayed, or depressed. And when we experience something pleasing, we can get similarly lost in ourselves, fixating on how great it is, how sad that it's not going to last, and, even as we are enjoying it, plotting to get more. We can feel guilty about pleasures, thinking that we don't deserve them, and that we should instead be giving our money to charity or helping homeless people instead of eating cake, watching television, or drinking a glass of wine.

The point of universalizing isn't to overindulge, then do some Buddhist practice to make up for our gluttony. But still, we do experience pleasures each day. This practice helps to make pleasure and pain part of our spiritual path, allowing us to weather our setbacks and enjoy our pleasures without the disturbing emotions of craving, aversion, and guilt.

Universalizing when things go your way

In learning to do this practice, first consider a simple pleasure. If you enjoy drinking coffee, you can imagine that you have just been handed a cup of it, made precisely the way you like it. Instead of swallowing it selfishly, sipping it with guilt, or throwing it away in disgust, the technique of universalizing is to simply enjoy it. But as you savor each sip, in your imagination, offer that pleasure to everyone in the world.

Grandly fantasize that, instead of you alone, 8 billion other people are enjoying this cup of coffee at the same time. You don't have to feel guilty (nor do you need to neurotically plan your next trip to the café). Simply find yourself in the present and use whatever experiences of pleasure you have to open your heart to others.

You can go into great detail in your imagination, offering specifically to those who are thirsty, starving, or poor. Think how much you would love to share this pleasure with them, nourishing them if you could.

Obviously, this practice doesn't give you permission to start eating, drinking, shopping, binge-watching, and hooking up in excess as you "offer it to all beings." Universalizing isn't a license for overindulgence, and we can remember Lorne Ladner's admonition that fake compassion is narcissism. But the focus in this first part of universalizing practice is on transforming your everyday pleasures, like lunch, work, fun, and friends, into a cause for greater love and compassion for others.

Universalizing when things go wrong
What about when things go wrong? The universalizing practice works with setbacks both trivial and heartbreaking: from your boss yelling at you to losing your job, from an unexpected bill to losing your home, from receiving the wrong order at a restaurant to not having enough money to buy food.

Instead of feeling angry, self-righteous, or defensive, consider how universalizing might help you soften and open your heart in such moments of pain. Starting small, imagine being criticized by your boss for a mistake at work. First, you can imagine millions of other human beings feeling similar pain. At this stage, the practice is like mindfulness, helping you to accept your feelings.

Then you go further, universalizing your pain so it becomes fuel for compassion. As you think of the many others who have the same pain as you right now, wish them to be free of it.

Often when things go wrong, you get angry and start fighting back, or you feel hurt as old wounds are reopened. Universalizing repurposes your own pain to connect you with the millions of other human beings feeling similar pain right now. In this case, you could think, "As my boss yells at me, may no one else be criticized, humiliated, disgraced, or insulted."

Then, you think of those who have it worse. This part can be tricky because you don't want to induce guilt, which can spiral into all sorts of bad feelings, like self-loathing or denial. But if your mind can handle it, try to measure your pain against other people's bigger problems. Compared to your work squabble, there are more extreme ways in which people are being insulted right now: imprisoned people subjected to constant abuse; immigrants denied asylum or separated from their children; people losing their jobs; people being unjustly accused of crimes; people whose partners are leaving them. Use your smaller pain to expand your heart to feel compassion for the greater pains that billions of other people are experiencing right now.

One of the most powerful things that I have found to universalize, apart from the difficult things that happen to me externally, is my inner delusions, thinking to myself, "May no one feel this strong craving" or "May no one feel so angry." Just realizing that others have the same delusions can be surprisingly effective in reducing our own.

Universalizing isn't a form of magical thinking that takes away anyone else's suffering in real life. But this mental practice helps you to enjoy life's fleeting pleasures more fully and accept its setbacks more gracefully. Universalizing turns every moment of your day into a means of expanding your compassion.

UNIVERSALIZING MEDITATION

The alchemical practice of "universalizing" transforms any experience into love and compassion. It helps counteract feeling hopeless or angry when things go wrong, and feeling selfish, guilty, or arrogant when things go well. You find a stable state of mind that remains calm and open through both pleasure and pain.

The meditation for universalizing is relatively simple:

- When you experience pleasure, imagine sharing it with everyone else who might enjoy it too.
- When you experience a difficulty, wish for those suffering similarly to be free from it.

UNIVERSALIZING YOUR PAIN

Start by transforming pain. Bring to mind a time when something challenging happened to you—breaking up, losing your job, falling ill, being blamed. Try to think of a time that you didn't respond well—when you got angry, felt jealous or resentful, or held a grudge.

Imagine yourself back in that situation and rehearse universalizing the experience to generate compassion for those who are enduring pain similar to yours or even worse.

- If your partner is breaking up with you, you can think, "May no one be separated from those they love."
- If you are losing your job, think, "May no one be deprived of their livelihood."
- If you are sick, think, "May no one fall ill and everyone who is sick be healed."
- If you are criticized, think, "May no one experience injustice, imprisonment, torture, or execution."

Think of other difficult experiences you've gone through and imagine universalizing them, too, as a way to expand your compassion, wishing that others be free from the suffering you have experienced.

UNIVERSALIZING YOUR PLEASURE

Now bring to mind a moment when you felt attachment while enjoying one of life's pleasures—eating a favorite treat, listening to great music, receiving an honor or promotion, feeling sexual pleasure. There's nothing wrong with enjoying pleasure. It only becomes destructive when you pursue it with addiction, craving, or obsession.

Next, imagine universalizing that experience, offering it to all beings. May all beings enjoy delicious food. May all beings enjoy their favorite music. May everyone find their perfect job and be appreciated for what they do. May all beings be held with tenderness by someone they love.

It can be especially helpful to think of those less fortunate than you and offer them the pleasures you enjoy. Sit silently with whatever pleasure you've chosen and offer it to those who need it most.

You can also expand from worldly pleasures to the deeper causes of happiness by thinking, "May all beings have whatever helps them let go of pain and evolve toward compassion, whether it is loved ones, a teacher, free time, or a spiritual practice."

DEDICATION: UNIVERSALIZING IN EVERYDAY LIFE

The point of universalizing in meditation is to put it into practice in daily life. Set an intention that, as you are eating lunch, you remember to think, "May all beings be nourished and have delicious food." And as you catch a cold, stub your toe, or your bank account runs low, remind yourself to think, "May all beings be free from illness, violence, and poverty."

12

STAGE 8, PART 1: HOW THINGS EXIST

One of my favorite movie scenes of all time occurs in the 1968 François Truffaut film *Stolen Kisses*, when its young hero, Antoine Doinel, stands in front of a bathroom mirror repeating the name of his lover. After a while, he switches to the name of his childhood sweetheart, and then he moves on to his own name, maniacally reciting it louder and louder while glaring at his own reflection. Finally, he slaps himself out of his existential crisis to get on with his day. You may have done something like this yourself (though perhaps with less drama), repeating your name or some other word over and over until its meaning dissolved into an arbitrary sound.

When I was a child I had a similar crisis, though it had nothing to do with a girlfriend. I began by touching one hand with the other at the fingertips. "That's part of my hand," I thought. Then I moved on to the fingers, knuckles, and palm and thought, "These too." But when I reached my wrist, I asked myself, "Where does my hand end and my arm begin?" I had just started peeking into a microscope at cells and I wondered whether there was some difference between a hand cell and an arm cell, a clear line where one ends and the other begins. But even then, part of me knew there was no such line, leaving me uneasy as to whether I even had a hand at all if I couldn't find its boundary.

The most advanced topic in Buddhism is *emptiness*, and exercises like these are used to get a glimpse at how things truly exist. The Buddhist view of ultimate reality doesn't rely on mathematical equations, but instead uses simple logic to recognize the dynamic interdependence of reality. Naturalist

John Muir put this poetically when he said, "When we try to pick out anything by itself we find that it is bound fast by a thousand invisible cords that cannot be broken, to everything in the universe."

Like other English translations of Buddhist terms, "emptiness" inadequately conveys its profound truth. In fact, Buddhist teachers explain that a true understanding of emptiness transcends words entirely. *Shunyata* (shoon-yah-ta), the Sanskrit term for emptiness, is sometimes also translated as "voidness." But as you learn about the concept of emptiness, it becomes clear that its true meaning is nearly the opposite of its English definitions. "Emptiness" and "voidness" are associated with feelings of meaninglessness, pointlessness, and non-existence, which are not at all what the term means once you come to understand it.

I sometimes think "fullness" would be a better translation, as the Dalai Lama has eloquently explained, "Emptiness should be understood in the context of dependent arising and it should evoke a sense of fullness, of things created by causes and conditions. We shouldn't think that the self is something that is originally there and then eliminated in meditation. In fact, it is something that never existed in the first place."

The essence of the teaching on emptiness is that nothing exists independently from anything else. Nothing appears out of nowhere and everything arises due to an endless interdependent chain of causes and conditions. Emptiness is not a place or a force of nature, but an active process, a property of everything. And analyzing the empty nature of reality according to the logic of interdependence is said to be the ultimate antidote to our delusions of anger and craving.

It's not self-evident why being able to see the interdependent nature of reality would stop these delusions, but the theory is that clinging to objects as independent entities creates polarizing dualities that feed our attachment and anger. You need to feel a solid, separate you and a solid, separate object for these delusions to function. Reflecting on emptiness breaks down this exaggerated distinction between you and the things you crave or despise.

An analysis of interdependence begins by noticing how objects around us appear to our minds as singular entities with the capacity to bring us happiness or pain from their own side. When we fail to see through the illusion of our senses and ego, people and things appear as though they simply popped into existence for our own pleasure or annoyance. But things are *empty* of existing in this illusory way.

Like the other Buddhist topics, emptiness isn't something you simply learn and memorize. Similar to cooking, playing a sport, or practicing a scientific discipline, the knowledge of emptiness is useless if it isn't applied in everyday life. Also, meditation on emptiness won't work if you pursue it with personal gain as a motivation, because selfishness itself is at odds with the logic of interdependence.

Though emptiness reveals the independence of objects to be illusory, it doesn't negate the world, the people around us, our own existence, or the moral impact that even our smallest actions have on others. Emptiness merely shows that things exist in a richer, more interconnected way than they ordinarily appear. Seen accurately, emptiness serves to emphasize the power of the choices we make, the love we share, and the things we accomplish in the world, making us aware of the rippling effects our actions have on everyone and everything around us.

Dependent origination

One of the most powerful ways to understand emptiness is through the logic of *dependent origination*. Emptiness depends on an object. It doesn't stand apart from objects or from the minds observing them. You choose to analyze the emptiness of a particular object, like a cup or a table. Then you start breaking it down into its parts through analysis: the cup's handle and the clay it's made from, the table's top and legs.

An object I personally like to analyze in this practice is one that you probably have in your pocket right now: a smartphone. I choose it not only because most of us are so attached to our phones but also because it turns out that a phone contains almost every type of matter in the universe—seventy-five of the ninety-two naturally occurring elements.

Parts, causes, and mind

Unlike pinning down the terminology, the process of meditating on emptiness isn't difficult to explain. Dependent origination involves breaking down any object into its parts, causes, and the mind perceiving it:

- all objects can be broken down into their parts, and those parts can be further divided into their subparts
- none of an object's parts arises spontaneously but each comes about through a variety of causes and conditions
- your mind places a label on top of these collected parts, which it mistakenly perceives as a singular entity

Applying this analysis to the example of your phone, you can reflect on all its myriad parts and the many causes that brought them together—from factory workers assembling components to molten metals in the Earth's core. Atop these parts and causes, your mind applies the seemingly arbitrary label "phone" that describes the function these collected parts temporarily perform for human beings.

Permanent, partless, and independent

When you don't see reality through the lens of dependent origination, you experience the mistaken view of *inherent existence* that sees an object as permanent, partless, and independent:

- you mistakenly see the object as permanent and unchanging, as if it had no beginning or end

- you mistakenly see the object as partless, appearing to you as a single object instead of one composed of smaller parts
- you mistakenly see the object as independent, as though it arose from nowhere instead of depending on the innumerable causes and conditions that temporarily bring its parts together.

Again, using the example of your phone, you can witness these illusions at play. Despite being made of countless parts, you may have never thought of it as anything other than a singular "phone." In fact, we hold so solidly to the partless concept of our phones that, even when it gets smashed into pieces, we still call this collection of parts a "broken phone," instead of naming the parts that comprise it. We rarely think of how our phone was made, how it continues to change, and how it will eventually be destroyed. Instead, we hold to the illusion that it is permanent, without beginning or end, and independent, almost as if it arose from nowhere.

Science proves that reality is illusory

The mistaken view of permanent, partless, independent objects that seem to exist inherently is biased by our biology, experience, and culture. When we critically investigate the world through the unbiased lens of dependent origination, we reveal the ultimate reality of emptiness, which in Buddhism is not only a philosophical position, but one bolstered by scientific evidence.

Scientists have conclusively demonstrated that physical reality is made up of parts—at its most subtle level, invisible vibrating particles and energy. And the psychological basis of our perceived reality is backed up by scientists' understanding that our senses experience reality through electromagnetic forces, which have no inherent color, visual form, sound, taste, tactility, or scent. The pale blue sky, a guitar's twang, honey's sweetness, and the texture of your lover's skin are all mental constructs.

Western scientists have understood this psychological basis of perception for centuries. As Europeans began to investigate the material underpinnings of reality in the seventeenth century, geniuses like Sir Isaac Newton and René Descartes all came to similar conclusions, recognizing that things exist in a way that is quite different from how they appear to us in everyday life. Galileo Galilei put it succinctly when he wrote, "I think that tastes, odors, colors, and so on reside in consciousness. Hence if the living creature were removed, all these qualities would be annihilated."

Ironically, the most advanced form of meditation in Buddhism is the one that may be easiest to root in science. And the Dalai Lama himself says that he now spends half his daily emptiness meditation on the modern view of quantum physics, which has shown with incredible precision how things don't appear to us as they truly are.

Concepts are empty too

Dependent origination argues for the interdependence of material objects. But it supports immaterial concepts just as well. I first heard the logic for this from the Dalai Lama when he explained how comparative extremes like hot and cold can't exist independently. There is no absolute hot, but only a hot in relation to something cooler. Similarly, tall and short are not inherent qualities of objects: a taller object depends on a shorter one to measure it against.

Cheap and expensive are also good examples: cheap compared to what? There's no such thing as cheap or expensive without relating the cost and quality of one thing to another. (By the way, be careful when having this debate with your partner—my wife hates it when I make metaphysical arguments about our finances.)

Analyzing the dependent origination of concepts can help in polarizing times, like those we are living through today. Liberals and conservatives are interdependent, existing only in relationship to one another. The definitions of liberal and conservative also depend on where you live and who you are talking to. The most conservative elected official in my home city of Berkeley, California, would be considered an arch-liberal in Scottsdale, Arizona. Liberals depend on conservatives for their very existence, just as conservatives depend on liberals. Each label makes no sense without the other to compare it to.

Concepts like moral, just, and beautiful are even more obviously empty. Every person on Earth would likely offer their own unique definitions, based on their biology, education, culture, and politics—not to mention the concepts of friend, enemy, and stranger, whose emptiness we meditated on in chapter 11.

Reality is not an illusion

Despite objects depending on parts, causes, and the minds perceiving them, this still in no way denies their existence entirely. *Conventional reality* does exist as the valid way objects normally appear to us, performing functions in the world and coming together through causes and conditions. Reality is not an illusion, but *illusory*, meaning that when we examine our perceived reality through the logic of dependent origination, conventional reality dissolves into the ultimate reality of emptiness, the rich, complex, and interdependent way that things truly exist.

So, when we say "empty," it is important to be precise about what objects, people, and ideas are empty of. They are empty of existing independent of their parts, the causes and conditions that bring them together, and the mind labeling this collection as a singular entity. They are not empty of existing entirely. A fire will still burn you if you stick your hand in it. And chocolate still tastes good—conventionally.

Meditating on emptiness isn't virtuous

A final point to reiterate about emptiness is that meditating on the ultimate nature of reality isn't, in itself, virtuous. If that were true, every particle physicist would be a saint. It's entirely possible to analyze reality in a clinical, intellectual, or even a malicious way, trying to understand the universe better so that you can manipulate it to suit your own selfish purpose—or even to harm others. Our ability to construct nuclear weapons based on our deepest material understanding of reality proves this to be true.

So if you want this practice to benefit your mind, before beginning an emptiness meditation, color your analysis on the nature of existence with a wish to become your most compassionate self and to create a better world.

MEDITATION ON HOW THINGS EXIST

This meditation on how things exist probes the deepest nature of reality to discover a healthier and more interdependent understanding of the things around you. It applies the logic of dependent origination to objects: how they are made of parts, how these parts come together through causes, and how your mind projects a label on to those caused parts, mistaking them as a singular, separate entity. The meditation explains how to perform this analysis for your phone, car, home, or meal. When you repeat the meditation later, you can apply the same reasoning to any object.

THE INTERDEPENDENT NATURE OF REALITY

Bring to mind an object to examine how it exists, ideally one you feel strong attachment to. Your phone is likely to be at hand, something you may get anxious about when you are parted from it for even a few minutes. Or you might choose your car, your home, or a favorite meal.

Once you have your chosen object of attachment in mind, first acknowledge that it does bring you conventional pleasure. It benefits your life in many ways and you can feel grateful for that.

Then dive deeper, to recognize some of the mistaken ways in which you ordinarily see the object.

Objects are made from parts

First, examine the parts of your object, seeing it more objectively, the way science tells us it exists. Start with the bigger, more obvious parts of the object. As you consider each one, ask yourself whether your phone, car, home, or meal can be found in it.

- Do you find your phone in its screen, microprocessors, battery, or buttons?
- Do you find your car in its wheels, chassis, engine, or windows?
- Do you find your home in its foundations, framing, floors, or walls?
- Do you find your food in its ingredients, like the flour, sugar, milk, eggs, or butter in a piece of cake? Individually, are these each as appealing as when they are mixed together?

Now imagine taking away one of your object's parts and replacing it with an identical one—swapping your phone's screen, your car's tires, or your front door. Would it still be the same object?

Then go more deeply.

- Examine the phone's resistors, capacitors, wires, and sensors.
- Consider the car's rubber, glass, plastic, steel, and aluminum.
- Think about the wood, wire, glass, brick, plaster, and concrete in your home.
- Imagine the plants and animals that make up your food—grains, chickens, cows, fruits, nuts, and vegetables.

Do you come closer to finding the essence of your object in any of these parts?

Now go even deeper, to the atomic level, considering the elements these objects are made from.

- Your phone contains nearly all the naturally occurring elements in the periodic table—oxygen, aluminum, magnesium, sodium, tin, and potassium in its touchscreen display; phosphorus, antimony, arsenic, boron, indium, and gallium in its processor; gold, silver, and copper wires, and tantalum capacitors; yttrium, europium, terbium, and gadolinium to color the pixels of its display; lithium, cobalt, and nickel in the battery; praseodymium and neodymium to drive its speakers and motors.
- A car is made from fewer elements—aluminum in the body and wheels; iron, bismuth, calcium, and carbon in its steel; chlorine, hydrogen, and oxygen in its plastics; gold and copper wires; panels and parts infused with helium and magnesium; platinum in the catalytic converter.
- Your home is made from mostly natural materials— wood comprised of carbon, hydrogen, oxygen, and nitrogen; pipes, wires, and nails made of copper, iron, gold, and aluminum; plaster made from calcium,

sulfur, oxygen, and hydrogen; paints containing zinc, oxygen, sulfur, and titanium.
- Food is made mostly from carbon, oxygen, nitrogen, and hydrogen spiced with bits of phosphorus, sodium, sulfur, and calcium.

Step back and imagine your object decomposed into vats and piles of its elements:

- seventy-five tiny mounds of granulated matter spread across your desk—one for each of the elements that make up your phone
- bigger piles of the dozen elements that make up your car heaped where it once was parked
- the many tons of elements that make up your home— vats of carbon, copper, iron, aluminum, and calcium; canisters of hydrogen, oxygen, and nitrogen
- your dinner plate with neat piles of carbon, phosphorus, sodium, sulfur, and calcium, paired with glass vials of oxygen, nitrogen, and hydrogen—how delicious would that seem?

For a minute, try to feel the same level of attachment to these piles of elements that you do to your object.

Imagine one further step down, to the subatomic level, where there is no longer color, form, taste, touch, or sound. See your phone, home, car, or meal as a buzzing cloud of energy, particles zipping through space.

Then zoom back to the conventional level, where the illusion of your phone, car, home, or meal again appears to your senses.

Causes bring parts of objects together
Now think about the causes that brought the parts of your object together.

• Imagine the people who designed your phone, and those who manufactured its components and transported them by air, ship, or truck between dozens of countries.

• Imagine where all the raw materials in your home or car were made and how they came together; who designed, grew, melted, cut, and hauled them around the world?

• With your meal, think about the people who planted the crops, watered and fertilized them, sold and resold them, processed, cooked, and delivered them to arrive in your refrigerator—and belly.

Think further back, through the history of science and technology, agriculture and commerce, and even society itself, that made the cultivation and collection of these raw materials possible. Think back to the evolution of intelligent life on Earth, which led to human beings being able to work together to make things. Think back to the dawn of life 4 billion years ago.

Think back to the birth of our star and solar system, then back further still to the explosion of earlier stars, which led to the formation of the heavy elements like carbon and oxygen that make up most of life on Earth. Think all the way back to the dawn of the universe, when the simpler elements like hydrogen, helium, and lithium were formed. See how your object is connected to the entire history of space and time.

And it is still connected right now. Each particle in your object feels the gravitational pull of every other particle in the universe and interacts electrochemically with others nearby.

The mind that labels caused parts

Now look at the role of your mind in shaping reality. See how it imposes on to this constantly changing continuity of parts (and the causes that brought them together) the labels of phone, car, home, or meal. Without your mind applying these labels, each would be only a loose collection of parts.

Imagine how other people and other creatures see your object differently from the way you do. They may not feel as strongly about your object. They may not care about it at all.

THINGS STILL EXIST CONVENTIONALLY

Now that you see your object in this more interdependent, changing way, recall again how you mistakenly see it as unchanging, partless, and independent. Does your ordinary perception now seem superficial compared to the rich way that things actually exist? You might even smile at this illusion you impose on reality.

By seeing reality this way, are your strong feelings of attachment reduced? Does the illusion of an independent object with the power to bring you pleasure or pain give way to a lighter, more interdependent way of seeing the world?

DEDICATION: ULTIMATE REALITY IN EVERYDAY LIFE

As you come out of the meditation, try to keep seeing the world through the lens of dependent origination, especially when strong feelings of attachment or aversion arise. Try to see through the illusion of a solid, separate, unchanging object to the changing, interdependent, energetic field that it truly is. Your mind only temporarily imposes a label on it of home, phone, car, or meal.

Practical emptiness

In case you are still scratching your head as to why meditating on your lunch ingredients will lead to a happier life, I want to end with an example of how meditating on emptiness has helped me personally.

More than a dozen years ago, during the Great Recession, I was running a company that created interactive exhibits for science museums. We were hit hard by the financial crisis, lost almost all our business, and had to lay off 80 percent of our staff. Not only that, but I was suddenly saddled with a huge amount of personal debt that I had little hope of ever paying off. I felt a great deal of both rational fear and irrational panic.

I tried all sorts of analytical meditation techniques to weather this tough time. And what most helped me slog into the office day after day to face personal ruin was the logic of emptiness.

Each day, on the long walk to work, I would go through the analysis of dependent origination. I tried to "find" the company that was causing me so much misery. Could I find it in the building, the people who worked there, its customers or products, the company's empty bank accounts, or the legal paperwork that established the corporation?

Each time I failed to find the company in any of its parts, my mind eased up on the catastrophic story I was telling myself. I saw that the situation was more flexible than it seemed, subject to change, causes, and conditions.

These thoughts helped me get through hundreds of scary days one by one. Emptiness didn't magically pay off the company's debts, but each day it helped me to avoid breaking down in despair. It gave me enough mental stability to keep working hard, stay open to the people around me, and remain creative and mentally flexible. Eventually I was even able to daydream about new ideas and I realized that I could release three old art projects as apps in Apple's new App Store and they became surprise hits. That led, the next year, to an incredible project, working with the Icelandic singer Björk. And that, in turn, led to founding a new, more successful company.

I'm not saying that meditating on emptiness will cause Björk to send you an email. But, sooner and in ways none of us expected, brighter days came for my whole team through opportunities we wouldn't have had if I had instead collapsed in a nervous breakdown.

Of course, meditating on emptiness only offers inner stability, not outer success. But at life's most challenging times, I have found it powerful to remember the words of emptiness's great exponent, Nagarjuna, "For whom emptiness is possible, everything is possible."

13

STAGE 8, PART 2: WHO AM I?

The French film character I mentioned in chapter 12 who couldn't stop saying his name may have suffered a momentary existential crisis, but I've had a more substantial problem my whole life, because I never identified with my name at all. To me, the name "Scott" feels more like a professional baseball player than the artist/inventor/philosopher I always fancied myself to be. "Scott" can't be shortened into a nickname and it has no meaning apart from "person from Scotland," where neither I nor my Jewish and German ancestors ever set foot.

I don't think my parents thought I felt like a "Scott" either because, when I was born, they failed to name me at all. That's why my birth certificate reads simply, "Boy Snibbe." When city officials grew impatient with my parents, it was my eleven-year-old uncle who finally chose my name. And, as far as I know, he *did* name me after a baseball player, since at the time he was obsessed with collecting baseball cards.

I almost changed my name when I went to college, but decided not to in the end, to rebel against my parents, who both changed their names after getting divorced. But keeping my name has meant that, whenever I'm introduced, I still kind of laugh at myself, with a sportsman's forename and a last name like an expletive—a word you might shout at the top of your lungs at someone who stole your phone: "Snibbe!"

But not identifying with the label that was placed on me has helped a lot in life, because there is a part of me that never quite took myself seriously. And this type of doubt about life's conventions turns out to be the starting point for meditating

on the emptiness of self—the most important "object" to
deconstruct when combatting our destructive delusions.

Who are you?

Do you feel that your name suits you? If not, do you identify
with some other label? "Who am I?" is one of the most
interesting questions you can ask yourself. So, before looking
at who you are from the perspective of the Buddhist teachings
on ultimate reality, take a moment to close your eyes and
answer this question without preconceptions.

What did you find? Did you identify with your body or
brain, your race, gender, religion, or country? Did you decide
that you are defined by some mark you've made in the world—
your work or your children, or the joys you've shared with
family, friends, and lovers?

You don't have to admit this to anyone, but perhaps deep
down you believe that you are your soul, an immaterial
spirit that moves from this life to an eternal afterlife; or a
reincarnated *atman*, the Hindu eternal self that travels from
body to body across lifetimes on Earth.

As a citizen of the information age, you may have decided
that you are the accumulation of your thoughts, feelings, and
knowledge. Some people not only believe this but also maintain
that the sum collection of their brain's connections and neural
activity could one day be uploaded to a digital brain in a virtual
world to live on forever in a technological hereafter.

The dependent origination of the self

In chapter 12, you meditated on how objects mistakenly
appear to exist as solid, separate, and unchanging. You broke
down that illusion by seeing through to the ultimate reality of
emptiness: how an object has no independent existence of its
own, but is merely labeled by your mind in dependence upon
parts that came together through myriad causes. This is the

logic of dependent origination, which accords with a scientific view of reality.

But meditating on the dependent origination of your phone or meal is just a warm-up for applying the same analysis to yourself. In Buddhism, all your disturbing emotions trace back to the root delusion of ignorance—a sense of separateness that causes attachment and anger to arise. These delusions are elaborated further, becoming jealousy, pride, competitiveness, addiction, and dozens of others.

To counteract these delusions, you first notice how you habitually project on to your collection of body and mind the same separate, solid, unchanging self-existence that you mistake in objects. Then, in meditation, you break through this false way your self appears to recognize that you are a collection of interdependent changing parts arising from causes and conditions, which your mind merely labels as "you."

Emptiness and compassion

Breaking through your sense of a separate self is supposed to lead to a happier, more meaningful life. But how? In Mahayana Buddhism, the teaching is that emptiness alone isn't capable of bringing you lasting happiness—it needs to be mixed with compassion. Combining emptiness and compassion is so critical that they aren't seen as separate topics. Rather, each supports the other. Feeling separate from the people and things around you is said to be your biggest obstacle to compassion. And thoughts of compassion demolish the alienated separateness you feel from those people and things.

Because of our ignorance, we cling to a strong, separate sense of self. We project on to others that they are the cause of our unhappiness. But believing that someone "annoys" us is only one of many possible stories we can tell ourselves. One way to meditate on emptiness is to analyze these stories. Put your opinion that someone is the cause of your problems front and center in your mind and debate with that thought. Is it true?

When I do this analysis with my own unhappy feelings, I almost always realize that I'm blaming and projecting. Of course, there is some element of truth to my story: it is conventionally true, based on my own biases and personal history. But, ultimately, my story doesn't support the mental afflictions that I build on top of it.

When you meditated on the emptiness of objects, you saw how ignorance makes you believe that your feelings are caused by things that seem separate from you. You crave more of those that appear pleasing and fewer of the ones that seem annoying. But when you analyze the objects that you crave or detest—and fail to find them—it helps curb your attachment and aversion.

This is even more effective when meditating on the emptiness of your self because, how can a self you don't find feel insulted? And is the insult you think you heard a real slight? Does everyone see it that way? You project your hurt on to someone else, thinking, "You are the cause of me not getting what I want. You are making me unhappy." But when you analyze this, you find that it's not true. There is the reality of that person's actions, and then there is the story you build up on top of those actions.

By routinely searching for my self (both in and out of meditation), more and more I find that I'm less agitated in difficult circumstances. I feel less put upon, resentful, or angry. I recognize that whatever story I'm telling myself about what's happening is just one interpretation among the infinite possibilities of emptiness. I start to see that I am a tumbling loose collection of mental and physical parts in constant interaction with other bodies and minds, each of us seeing reality through our own biased lens.

It's not only Buddhists who have had this realization of the emptiness of the self. Albert Einstein once shared similar sentiments in a letter to a friend:

A human being is a part of the whole, called by us "Universe," a part limited in time and space. He experiences himself, his thoughts and feelings as something separated from the rest—a kind of optical delusion of his consciousness. This delusion is a kind of prison for us, restricting us to our personal desires and to affection for a few persons nearest to us. Our task must be to free ourselves from this prison by widening our circle of compassion to embrace all living creatures and the whole of nature in its beauty.

By closely examining his own inner and outer realities, Einstein discovered for himself the connection between emptiness and compassion. What Buddhism can offer on top of such inspiring insights is a method for systematically cultivating a realization of emptiness, helping you to grow a beautiful idea into something you instinctually feel in everyday life.

Emptiness is searching, not finding

Despite the rousing logic of the power of emptiness to free you from your delusions, it's okay to still feel skeptical that meditating on the emptiness of your self will release you from suffering. Accepting the invitation to try out Buddhist mind-training techniques does not require you to unthinkingly adopt a set of dogmas. Remember that the Buddha himself said to personally verify his teachings using critical reasoning, logic, and your direct experience in meditation.

The idea that ignorance of the true nature of reality is the root of your suffering is one you can take as a hypothesis. To prove whether emptiness really is an antidote to your suffering, it's essential to meditate again and again on the mistaken way that things appear conventionally—in this case, your self. This is where even secular forms of Buddhism diverge from science, because, after the relatively simple process of convincing yourself of the logic of dependent origination, your primary task is to explore a direct experience of emptiness that can't yet be measured by any scientific instrument.

Furthermore, you may experience the beneficial results of meditating on the emptiness of the self without ever coming to a conclusion about what the self is. One of the most profound aspects of meditating on emptiness is that it is a continual process of searching—in which you may never find what you are looking for. You search for the independent, annoying self that gives you so much grief, then ask if that person truly exists in the way it seems. The question may be more important than any answer.

Three types of self

It took me a long time to gather (and at least partially understand) the precise teachings on how to meditate on the emptiness of self, and I want to explain some details that are rarely shared with a general audience. The meditation at the end of this chapter guides you through all these details experientially without the need to memorize any terms. But knowing the terminology used to think about the self can help you better understand it, just as the terminology about the mind in chapter 4 helps you to calm and steer it.

The Tibetan Buddhist *middle way* philosophy describes three ways that people can view their "I," or self. These progressively subtler ways of seeing the self help us understand our different levels of self-deception: the *inherent "I,"* the *conventional "I,"* and the *merely labeled "I."* The merely labeled "I" is the accurate one, a self "merely labeled" on the basis of its physical and mental parts and the causes that bring them together. The conventional "I" is the most common one that we experience in everyday life, present when we are free from strong emotions that make us feel disconnected from the world around us. And the inherent "I" is the one we have when caught up in delusions, believing in a strong sense of self that is separate from (and often opposed to) other people and things.

In describing our deluded sense of self, we use the same terminology that we did in relation to objects, misapprehending ourselves to be permanent, partless, and independent in the following ways.

- When we see ourselves as *permanent*, we are unaware that we were conceived and born, we will one day die, and our bodies and minds, even now, are continually changing.
- When we see ourselves as *partless*, we fail to recognize that we are a bundle of countless trillions of parts, with muscles contracting, organs processing, blood flowing, neurons firing, cells metabolizing, and particles exchanging energy. We also have an illusion of a partless mind—a singular sense of "I, me, mine."
- When we see ourselves as *independent*, we feel separate from the people and planet around us. We fail to see the infinite web of causes and conditions—material, biological, and social—that bring us into being and that we depend on for our existence.

Together, these mistaken views are manifestations of ignorance—the root delusion described in earlier chapters as "selfishness," but now better described as "selfness." Ignorance makes us believe in a permanent, partless, independent self—the inherent "I."

Something interesting about this view of an illusory self that strongly believes in I, me, and mine, and gets angry and attached, is that it is not always there. When we are going about our day, absorbed in a task like making dinner or taking a walk, our strong sense of self can fade away. This weaker sense of self is called the conventional "I." Even if we have not realized its emptiness, this self is not much of a problem and isn't strongly deluded.

The most accurate merely labeled "I" is the one experienced by those who have realized emptiness, which we gradually get more and more of a taste of in meditation. The curious thing about meditating on the dependent origination of the self is that you have to make the more annoying inherent "I" appear in order to break down its illusion. But given how often this irritating self manifests for the average person, you will probably find it just as easy to conjure up as I do. One way is to think of a time when you were strongly criticized. Another is to remember a moment of strong attachment or anger. If you are sufficiently mindful, you can become aware of the inherent "I" amid everyday conflict or craving, then stop right there and apply the analysis of dependent origination to dismantle its illusion.

But the first step in meditating on the emptiness of the self is to allow this independent, inherent "I" to arise. Once it's there, perform the three-part dependent origination analysis on this false sense of self to understand how it depends on parts, causes, and mind. You then search for that inherent self, which seems to exist from its own side, independent from the continually changing parts of your body and your continually changing stream of mental experiences.

The five aggregates

The method used to search for the self among its parts is based on one of the Buddha's most famous teachings, called the *five aggregates*. This is a way of breaking down your person into its physical body—*form*, the first aggregate—plus four mental aggregates: *feeling, perception, mental formations*, and *consciousness*.

The first two of these mental aggregates are mental factors that you meditated on in chapter 4: feeling, your reaction of pleasant, unpleasant, or neutral to anything you perceive; and perception, your mind's ability to wrap a bundle of sense phenomena as a singular object or concept. Mental formations include a collection of numerous other mental factors including contact, attention, and urge, your movement to action. Consciousness, which you also experienced in chapter 4's nature of mind meditations, is the last of the aggregates, awareness itself.

Though you perform the same dependent origination analysis you used on objects when meditating on the emptiness of the self, there is an important distinction between objects and living beings because, unlike objects, living beings have minds that offer them independence and agency. So the analysis of the emptiness of a person needs to not only consider the parts and causes of the body but also analyze the parts and causes of the mind to see how it, too, is empty.

The causes of the mind

In chapter 7, you meditated on the causes of your body and physical objects, but not the causes of the mind. However, when meditating on selflessness, you now reflect on the various causes you find for your mind, searching for your self among them.

You can start with the more obvious causes of ideas and concepts. Every word you know was invented by someone else. Your parents and teachers taught you about the world and society. Books, the media, and schools also shaped who you are. Every single experience you've ever had in this life helped to form your unique mind, along with evolution, your brain's wiring, and the physical laws of the universe.

As you analyze the causes of your mind and its ever-changing moments of consciousness, you may take the view that your mind is determined entirely by the neurons in your brain and their electrical activity. This is a scientific materialist point of view, and it can be as fruitful as any other in deconstructing the self, because neuroscientists have shown that when people reflect on their sense of self, the brain activates in many different areas and in different patterns for different people at different times. There is no "self" organ in the brain, no control center that lights up when you have a strong sense of "I." So if your self is your brain, it can't be isolated to any one of its parts.

There is another Buddhist doctrine to consider, which is that the cause of one moment of consciousness is simply the previous one. It's worth taking this on as a hypothesis in meditation, simply to examine it, because it provides a subtle way to understand your mind's "software." Even a computer's software isn't wholly determined by its hardware but, instead, evolves by combining its prior computational state with the rules of its program and new inputs. That next state is stored in the computer's hardware but is not that hardware itself. If you believe the mind works like a computer, the Buddhist explanation that the immediate cause of a moment of consciousness is the prior one may make a lot of sense. To turn this thought experiment into a meditation on the emptiness of your mind, you then actively search for your self in each new moment of consciousness that was caused by the prior one.

These are only some of the ways that you can think about the causes of your mind. In searching for the self, you can use your creativity, intelligence, and education to continue asking openly, what are the causes of consciousness?

You do exist

Before detailing the meditation on the emptiness of self, it's worth repeating a warning usually given to emptiness meditators: don't let this analysis slide into the nihilistic view that you don't exist at all or that your actions have no consequences. This was the mistake I made as a child, wondering whether my hand even existed if I couldn't find its boundary with my arm. You *do* exist, but the *way* you exist is so much more expansive, profound, and inclusive than you may have ever imagined.

You discover the dependently originated self by analyzing the independent-seeming self—the inherent "I." Although the inherent "I" doesn't exist, it still habitually appears to us, just as we might mistake one person for another. Through analyzing the inherent "I" we reveal the more accurate merely labeled "I" which is entirely interdependent: the coming together of the body's physical and mental parts through myriad causes and conditions, which the mind merely labels as "me."

All these explanations may sound quite technical, but the point of meditating on the emptiness of the self is to find a more expansive sense of being that is interconnected, open, and joyful rather than separate, solid, and unhappy.

MEDITATION ON SEARCHING FOR THE SELF

Meditating on the emptiness of the self breaks down the root delusion of ignorance: seeing ourselves as separate from the people and things around us, with the illusion that we are singular beings who have unchanging identities. This self-centered delusion gives rise to attachment and anger at the people and things that seem separate from us, and is said to be our greatest obstacle to happiness and connection.

THE FIVE AGGREGATES OF THE SELF
To dismantle the inaccurate sense of a separate self, the Buddha taught a method of breaking that self down into five aggregates. The first aggregate of form is your body. The other four aggregates relate to your mind, categorizing it into feeling, perception, mental formations, and consciousness.

CONJURING THE INHERENT "I"
When you meditate, the separate-feeling self often isn't there because you are in a relaxed state of mind, focused on beneficial thoughts. You have to work at conjuring this inaccurate sense of self in order to refute it.

Bring to mind a time when you were criticized. If you can remember being falsely criticized, that's even better—a time when a strong sense of self welled up in you—an "I" who felt wronged.

Now start to examine this indignant "I," searching among its parts for a self who feels partless, unchanging, and independent.

SEARCHING FOR THE SELF IN THE BODY

First, look for this inherent self in your body. Is that self who feels criticized in your feet, legs, torso, liver, heart, or lungs? Can you find it in your kidneys, stomach, arms, or hands? Do you find this inherent "I" in the doors to your senses—your eyes, ears, nose, tongue, or skin?

Or do you find this separate self in your brain? If so, in which part? On the left side or the right? In any single neuron or in all of them?

Do you find this "I" in the blood circulating through your body, or in any of your body's cells? Is the inherent "I" found in the electrical signals passing through your neurons? Can you find yourself in your DNA or your microbiome's billions of cooperating bacteria?

Do you find yourself in your molecules? Are you the water that your body is mostly made of, or the electrolytes, carbohydrates, lipids, proteins, and vitamins suspended in it?

Are you the oxygen, carbon, hydrogen, nitrogen, calcium, and phosphorous in your molecules, the building blocks of biochemistry?

Are you the subatomic particles in those atoms—the electrons, protons, and neutrons exchanging at near light speed among your body's matter? Or quarks, leptons, and bosons? Are you these fundamental building blocks of the universe?

We know from quantum mechanics that matter exists in a probabilistic state in which particles flicker in and out of existence within the spaciousness of an atom's field. Is your self these probabilistic appearings and vanishings or the space within which they appear?

SEARCHING FOR THE SELF IN FEELING

Now search for the separate self in your mind. First make sure that annoying, indignant self is still there to search for. If not, think again of a time when you felt wronged.

Then probe the mental factor of feeling. Are you the pleasant feelings you have when you hear kind words, see beautiful sights, or smell and taste delicious food? Are you the good feelings that arise through your skin and muscles in response to affection and exercise, or those that come from pleasant thoughts or memories?

Do you find this self in unpleasant feelings—when you are uncomfortable, or in pain, criticized, attacked, blamed, or ignored?

Or does your separate-feeling self identify with the neutral feelings of indifference you have when passing a stranger or being served by an assistant at a store?

SEARCHING FOR THE SELF IN PERCEPTION

Perception is the part of your mind that applies a label to bundles of sensory experience: carbohydrates and proteins on a clay plate as your dinner; plant cells as a flower; metal, glass, and microprocessors as your smartphone.

Are you your mind's capacity to label invisible particles and electromagnetic energy as colors, forms, sounds, tastes, smells, and touches; as dinner, flower, phone, or me?

SEARCHING FOR THE SELF IN MENTAL FORMATIONS

Do you find yourself in any of your other mental factors: your senses making contact with the outer world, your attention to some things more than others, your powerful urges to speak or act, to go beyond thinking to doing?

Or are you all the complicated thoughts and feelings that follow, like jealousy, pride, love, compassion, even yearnings for equality or justice?

SEARCHING FOR THE SELF IN CONSCIOUSNESS

Now search for your self in your consciousness, through which mental factors flow. Relax into the space of your mind. Does it feel vast or confined, luminous or dark, clear or obscured? Does it reflect and know what appears to it?

Direct your attention away from the mental factors that come and go in your mind and toward wherever they emerge from and dissolve back into. What is that ground from which they appear?

If you experience some intuitive sense of your mind's nature, relax into it. Is this the ultimate place where you finally find the inherent "I," here in the space of the mind?

If you decide you are this non-conceptual space, investigate further. Divide the space of the mind in two. Is this "I" in one half or the other? Subdivide your mental space into little cubes. Do you find yourself in any one of them, or in the collection?

The mind changes over time. Moments of consciousness arise, grow, sustain, diminish, and disappear. Some contain thoughts, while others are the direct experience of the mind itself.

Do you find your self in any one moment of consciousness, perhaps the one happening right now? If so, what happens to that self when the current moment disappears? Is it left behind with that prior moment of consciousness? Does the self jump to the next? Or is the self separate from any moment of consciousness?

Since moments of consciousness have a duration, you can split them into earlier and later moments. When you do this, do you find your self in one, the other, or both?

If you keep slicing moments of awareness, do you eventually find an indivisible quantum of consciousness? Or can you divide moments of consciousness forever? What happens when a slice of consciousness becomes infinitely thin? Does the self disappear? Or does it become something that transcends time altogether?

SEARCHING FOR THE SELF IN CAUSES

The physical and mental parts of your self all have causes. Can you find yourself in any of them?

Thich Nhat Hahn says that you are only made of non-you elements. Your body began with the sperm and egg of your parents, then took in nutrients to grow within your mother and, later, outside her. As you grew, you kept turning "non-you" elements into "you" and have done so ever since, up until the last meal you ate and the last breath you took.

Teachers, parents, and friends taught you every word and concept you know. Your skills, beliefs, and opinions came from others too.

Trace your body and mind back through the 10,000 generations of humans who created the languages, civilizations, technologies, and religions that brought you to where you are today.

Trace back further through millions of years of evolution, from apes, mammals, and fish to tiny sea creatures and bacteria. Trace all the way back to the origin of life on Earth 4 billion years ago.

All the energy on Earth comes from our 4.5-billion-year-old star. And all the elements that make up life on Earth came from earlier stellar explosions that forged carbon, nitrogen, and the other heavy elements of life. Ultimately, your physical body traces back to the big bang, to the beginning of matter, energy, and even time itself.

Come back to the present and realize how, even now, every atom in your body is moved by the gravitational attraction of every other particle in the universe. Galaxies billions of light years away exert a tiny influence on every particle of your body. Even now, you are interconnected with the entire universe.

THE MIND AND SELF

What role does your mind play in constructing the self? You are a collection of an uncountable number of parts, brought together by innumerable causes stemming back to the origin of the universe. On top of these caused parts, your mind applies the label of your name. You may identify with it so strongly that you feel a surge of excitement or fear when someone says it out loud. But you are not your name. Your name is just a label placed on your caused parts.

Imagine seeing yourself this way in daily life—interdependent, constantly changing, made of countless parts produced by an infinite stream of causes and effects. If you could always see yourself this way, how would you respond to criticism, blame, craving, or praise? Who is criticized, blamed, or praised? Who is craving or afraid? Am I even the same person who was praised or blamed just seconds ago?

BEYOND CONCEPTS

Now let go of the analysis. Let go of concepts. Let go into a non-conceptual understanding of yourself that transcends identifying with any one part of your body or mind or the collection of mental and physical parts. Relax into an interdependent sense of being that transcends ego or labels to know yourself, perhaps for the first time, as you truly are.

DEDICATION

Eventually, return to concepts. You exist. You haven't negated yourself, you have simply expanded your understanding of your body and mind. The independent, unchanging, partless view of yourself is so limiting, narrow, and wrong.

Your feeling of separateness is just a misunderstanding of who you really are. Once you become aware of your interdependent, changing self, composed of countless physical parts and mental moments, this illusion becomes unnecessary. You are so much more than the lonely, detached, needy illusion that your ego imposes on you.

Yet, what this meditation reveals is that when your narrow, egotistic self arises, you can see such a moment as a gift: an opportunity to perform this magnificent analysis of how you truly exist. By questioning how that self appears, you embrace interdependence, awakening to your connection to all life, and everything else in the universe.

14

A SKEPTIC'S PATH TO ENLIGHTENMENT

My brother told me this story when he first started studying Buddhism. His teacher asked the students, "Do you know that feeling when you are about to say something and then you forget what you were going to say?" The teacher paused, everyone nodded, and then he continued, "Well, that's the feeling you want to have all the time!"

It may be too optimistic to think that simply forgetting what you were going to say will give you a glimpse of the ultimate nature of reality. But one way to describe the experience of emptiness is seeing things non-conceptually, without labels or even boundaries. "Seeing is forgetting the name of the thing one sees" is how the author Lawrence Weschler once put it.

Analytical meditation offers a rich path of thoughts and stories that eventually leads to realizations like these, transcending the words and ideas that helped you get there. So, as a final paradox, the main point of this chapter is to convince you to remember the conceptual lamrim topics so that the gateways they provide to non-conceptual realization are always at hand.

In chapter 1, I suggested meditating on each stage of A Skeptic's Path to Enlightenment for a week before going on to the next. That way, you go beyond the intellectual to directly experience how the stages of the path transform your mind. Once you have some experiential understanding of each topic that has come to you through meditation, a powerful way to practice next is to meditate on the entire sequence in a single session.

People who practice the lamrim in the Tibetan style often review the whole path as part of their daily meditation practice. I do this myself each day. When I don't have much time, this can take as little as a minute, in what's called a *glance meditation*. But, when I wake up early enough, this part of my practice can stretch leisurely into half an hour or more. Whether brief or extended, meditating on the entire path can be of great benefit, which is why, in this final chapter, I share a complete meditation that includes each of the topics for the eight lamrim stages. You will notice that there is some variation in how I have structured the stages. Analytical meditation is a creative activity, so you can experiment to find the approach that works best for you in the moment.

Memorizing the names of the topics for the stages is useful too: the precious life, impermanence, cause and effect, refuge, suffering, renunciation, compassion, and interdependence. The words themselves can rekindle whatever realization you have gleaned from your meditation. You can go through the sequence as you are walking down the street, in your car, or even when you wake up unexpectedly in the middle of the night. I find a midnight review of the lamrim is a much better use of my time than the restless worrying that used to consume me.

I've never heard anyone talk about this, but I have also noticed that sometimes when I go over the lamrim topics from memory, I inadvertently skip over one. When I catch myself making these mistakes, I often laugh, because I've usually skipped the topic that I needed to reflect on the most. For example, I skipped cause and effect when I was going against my own values. Or I skipped renunciation while caught up in strong craving.

You probably noticed that the different methods for exploring the nature of the mind recur repeatedly throughout the Skeptic's Path to Enlightenment sequence. That's why I don't separate out the mind to give it its own meditation stage. Instead, in any of the places where the mind comes up, you can choose to go deeper and spend more time meditating on its nature there, which also happens to be a great way to strengthen your concentration.

At the beginning of this book, I reflected on enlightenment as an ideal that helps to drive your life toward happiness, meaning, and connection. It goes without saying that I'm not enlightened, and this book's secular versions of lamrim meditations diverge from the Buddhist ones in key ways. However, I do feel confident that if you practice them sincerely, these meditations will lead to genuine realizations like those I and my students have had over the years, moving toward enlightenment's ideal of bringing out your best qualities and diminishing your delusions.

The main advantage of this sequence is that it doesn't require any beliefs that can't be proven by modern science. And even practicing Buddhists can benefit from these modern twists on ancient topics, because they honestly confront those elements of the path that Westerners find difficult to believe, and explore meaningful alternatives. Given my creative divergence from the Buddhist path, I suppose I should have called this sequence A Skeptic's Path to a Path to Enlightenment, but that's not as catchy!

I sometimes like to ask experienced Buddhist practitioners what enlightenment means to them personally. One of them gave me this answer: enlightenment is being able to do the right thing at the right time for the right reason. I think that's as much as any of us could wish for in life, and I hope this final meditation helps you come slightly closer to that ideal.

MEDITATION ON
A SKEPTIC'S PATH TO ENLIGHTENMENT

POSTURE
Settle yourself into a meditation posture, cross-legged on a cushion, or on a chair with your feet flat on the floor. Set your right hand over the left in your lap, palms up with the tips of your thumbs touching, eyes half closed, and your head slightly tilted down. Then let all the parts of your body relax.

MOTIVATION
Set a motivation for meditating today not only to relax but to better understand your mind; to steer your thoughts and actions toward the true causes of a happy, meaningful life; to become a source of happiness for the people around you; and to bring about a better world.

FOCUSING ON THE BREATH
Bring your attention to your breath, as it comes in and out of your nostrils or with the rise and fall of your abdomen. Notice how your breath is a sensory experience reflected in your mind. If other thoughts, feelings, or perceptions intrude as you focus on your breath, let them pass by. There's no need to push them away or to bring them closer. Remain focused on your breath for one minute.

THE PRECIOUS LIFE
You woke up today, alive in your remarkable body. If you have some degree of health, clean water, and you can read and write, you are more fortunate than billions of people on Earth. For a moment, feel grateful for these basic

endowments, then for more, if you have them: a place to live, money in the bank, a job, family, friends.

What can you accomplish in these next twenty-four hours? At the very least, you can be a source of comfort, help, and joy to those around you. And whether you succeed or not, having such a compassionate motivation becomes the cause of your own happiness.

You've also found an interest in going beyond mere survival, to probe the deep questions of existence itself. Expand your mind to think about your role in the universe. It took 4 billion years for life on our planet to evolve into a form that could reflect on itself, the nature of reality, and consciousness. What responsibility do we have as such highly evolved beings? What if humanity is unique, the only intelligent life in a universe of billions of galaxies, 13.8 billion years old? If that's true, how do you want to spend this day?

IMPERMANENCE

Look more deeply into what it means to be alive. Start by exploring your body's parts, resting your mind on each of them in turn:

- your feet, legs, and torso; your heart, liver, lungs, kidneys, stomach, and skeleton; your arms and hands
- the signals coming from your eyes, ears, nose, tongue, and fingers, through which your brain constructs a picture of reality
- blood circulating through your entire body once every minute
- trillions of individual cells, millions dying each second, with millions of new ones replacing them
- countless spinning atoms of hydrogen, oxygen, nitrogen, and carbon within those cells, exchanging subatomic particles at nearly the speed of light.

To be alive is to change in every instant.

Bring your mind to your cushion or chair, to the room around you and everything in it. Become aware that these are also changing and decaying at a subtle level instant by instant.

Then look inside your mind to observe how it changes. Thoughts and feelings arise, grow, sustain, diminish, and disappear—happiness, sadness, yearning, fear, pain, revulsion, joy.

The impermanent nature of your mind means that you can steer it in any direction, so why not direct it toward happiness, meaning, and benefiting others? Impermanence means anything is possible.

CAUSE AND EFFECT

Everything humans have achieved—agriculture, medicine, democracy, spaceflight—all of these started in the mind. Our minds can even transform the planet, as climate change proves.

Yet we often lose control of our minds and let anger and craving overtake us. Just because something pops into your head doesn't mean you must follow its urges or fears. Don't believe everything you think.

To gain control over your mind, start by simply becoming aware of what appears in it. See that you can maintain a distance from your thoughts, feelings, and perceptions. You can label them, but you don't need to react to them.

What are the causes of happiness and pain for your own mind and for the minds of others? Is it possible that humans mostly mean well and only cause harm through confusion and conditioning?

Search through your previous twenty-four hours alive for a time when you were at your best. Perhaps you cared for yourself in a moment of calm, exercise, or creativity; maybe you experienced a moment of connection when you helped someone by listening, working, or laughing together. Rejoice in your chosen moment and briefly determine to do more nourishing things like that today— for yourself and for others.

Now think of something you regret from the past day. See how that action didn't come out of the blue but stems from a long chain of causes and effects, external influences and inner habits that are reinforced every time you repeat them.

What could you have done instead? How could you have handled the situation better? Determine to act that way when it happens again. And if there are external influences that reinforce your habit, maybe it makes sense to avoid them.

If you haven't already, forgive yourself for whatever you regret. Let go of any guilt or shame and accept that change happens slowly. You can feel sincere remorse for whatever harm you have done in the world and move on with a clear mind and a heart open to others.

REFUGE

Who do you admire? Humanitarians, athletes, artists, activists; or humbler people in your everyday life who seem to think only of others?

Your ability to change not only means that you can steer your mind toward greater good but also that you even have the potential of a Dalai Lama, Wangari Maathi, Gandhi, or Martin Luther King Jr. The qualities these great beings cultivated in themselves can be developed by everyone. We all have the seeds of kindness, compassion, and wisdom. Mental disturbances like anger, craving, pride, and jealousy are fleeting and shallow. You can let them go simply by embracing your own capacity for good.

Whether you fully believe this or not, find refuge in your own inner goodness for a moment and in anyone you admire who embodies virtue. Find refuge in your capacity to change, and everyone else's capacity to change too. Watch how these thoughts affect who you are right now and how you see others.

SUFFERING

Although we experience endless varieties of suffering and conflict, the root of our mental pain lies in three delusions so strong that in Buddhism they are called poisons: attachment, anger, and ignorance. Simply becoming mindful of these disturbing mental states, labeling them and understanding them, is a huge step toward eliminating the pain they cause us, as we realize they are exaggerated, inaccurate ways of seeing reality.

Attachment

Remind yourself how attachment works. You perceive an object that pleases you: a delicious treat, the touch of someone's body, some status in the world. And then your mind externalizes that pleasure. You start to believe that you can't be happy without it. You must get it now—and keep getting it. If you don't, you can't be happy. Attachment exaggerates the capacity of people, objects, and experiences to bring you happiness.

When you get the object of your attachment, do you feel completely satisfied? Even if you do, does that feeling last? Watch your state of mind when you get the object of your attachment. Could it be that the reason you feel good is not because you satisfied your craving for some short time, but because you are, just for a moment, free from your attachment?

Anger

Anger is the opposite of attachment. You feel unhappy with an object or situation that displeases you. But anger takes you beyond the unpleasant situation; it causes you to project exaggerated negative qualities on to the thing itself. With people, this can cause you to exaggerate so badly that you fail to see any good at all in the person you are angry with.

Think of someone you are angry with right now to see if this is true. Notice how exaggerated your state of mind is. The person you are angry with probably isn't harming you or even thinking about you right now. That person may be caring for family or friends, or doing some good in the world—but still you feel angry at them. How accurate is your view that this person only does harm?

Ignorance

The root delusion of ignorance is seeing an exaggerated distinction between yourself and others. Through ignorance you fail to see the interdependent, changing nature of reality, instead creating the illusion of strong opposites—good and bad, delicious and disgusting, me and you.

This ignorance turns into self-centeredness as you start, absurdly, to think that you are a little bit more important (or less important) than everyone else in the universe. It's almost funny when you realize this—"I actually think I'm the center of the universe!" Ask yourself if your exaggerated sense of separateness and autonomy might be at the root of all your other forms of suffering. Try to see through this delusion to how you truly are—one among equals in a world of constantly changing interconnected bodies, matter, and minds.

RENUNCIATION

In letting go of the causes of suffering, do you need to renounce sensual pleasures, relationships, and even the invigorating conflicts that your delusions respond to? Is that the path to happiness?

True renunciation doesn't mean giving up small pleasures, like ice cream or hikes in the woods, or even giving up big ones, like making love to your partner, or the joys of family and friends. Renunciation isn't rejecting the beautiful, pleasurable, meaningful parts of life; it is letting go of the delusions you wrap around pleasant and difficult experiences. Those delusions are the attachment, anger, and self-centered ignorance that keep you from genuinely enjoying life's fleeting pleasures and weathering life's inevitable pains.

Are anger and attachment intrinsic to who you are? Imagine letting go of them. Free from craving, is it possible you might actually enjoy life more? Without anger, would your relationships be healthier and deeper?

Imagine letting go of a self-centered way of viewing the world. Imagine seeing things as changing and impermanent, from multiple perspectives, with the long view that a happy, stable mind is more important than being right or wrong, winning or losing.

LOVE AND COMPASSION

When you renounce your self-centered delusions, it's natural that your heart softens and your concern for others grows. You can expand these feelings with the practices of . equanimity, love, compassion, and rejoicing.

Equanimity

First, practice equanimity to equalize your bias. Think of a friend, enemy, and stranger side by side in front of you. See

how your labels of "friend," "enemy," or "stranger" come
from seeing only through your perspective. From their side,
each of them wants to be happy and doesn't want to suffer,
just like you.

Now look at them from the perspectives of others. To
some, each is a dear friend; to others, an enemy; and to
many more, a stranger.

Relationships also change. Remember friends who have
turned into enemies or strangers. Remember enemies who
have turned into friends. And remember how your friends
and enemies were all once strangers.

What would the world look like if we treated one
another equally? By realizing that relationships are relative
and impermanent, may my actions help to create a more
equitable world, where everyone is treated fairly.

Love
Once you've established the foundation of equanimity,
it's possible to go further—to wish everyone not only
their basic dignities but the abundance of good that we
all deserve.

Imagine the people you care about, gathered beside
and behind you—family, friends, colleagues. Wish them
happiness and the causes of happiness; may they have the
material things they need—money, shelter, safety. May they
be loved.

Now imagine your enemies gathered in front of you—
specific ones from your life and ones from the greater
world. They want to be happy too. If it's hard for you to
accept this, remember that, even from your own selfish
perspective, if your enemies were truly happy, they would
probably stop harming you and the people you care about.
Your enemies only cause harm because of their delusions,
believing that hurting others will somehow make them

happy. Wish your enemies happiness and even that you might be a cause of their happiness.

Then imagine how everyone else on the planet also deserves to be happy; deserves the dignities of food, shelter, health, and security; deserves to be loved. Imagine that everyone is given everything they need. And aspire that you may become a cause of their happiness.

Compassion

Just as everyone wants to be happy, no one wants to suffer. Think about your friends, family, and colleagues, and all they suffer through. Picture them beside and behind you and wish for them to be free from their suffering.

Imagine the millions of people who also suffer from similar problems, with health, money, grief, conflict, injustice, or mental illness. Wish for them to be free from their problems too.

Extend your compassion further to include the billions of people worldwide who face the severe difficulties of poverty, violence, racism, political oppression, being enslaved or sexually exploited. Think of all the awful suffering around the world and wish for everyone to be free from it.

Then bring to mind your enemies, who also don't want to suffer. They, too, face problems with their mind, health, and material conditions. Wish for your enemies to be free from suffering.

Rejoicing

Now recall all the kindness and good that your family, friends, and colleagues accomplished in the past twenty-four hours.

Think of all the good things that happened to people close to you: they heard kind words, they were hugged and held, they ate delicious, nourishing meals, they received wealth, recognition, and success, they felt loved and appreciated. Rejoice in all the good they enjoyed and feel that they deserve it.

In the same way, think about people you don't know but admire: religious leaders, compassionate politicians, humanitarians, activists, caregivers. Take a moment to rejoice in the great things they accomplished today that you either know of or can easily imagine, and all the good they experienced.

This is harder but, without feeling jealous or spiteful, try to also see the good in your enemies: the praise they received, their achievements, wealth, relationships, and whatever good they did today.

INTERDEPENDENCE

Now examine who you are with intelligent curiosity. Try to remember a time you were criticized or felt strong anger or craving. This activates that exaggerated sense of "I" that feels separate and self-centered.

Move through the parts of your body, like you did while meditating on impermanence. But now, as you imagine your body's organs, cells, molecules, and particles, for each part, ask yourself if you find that separate self in any of them.

You can stop longer at the brain if you find yourself there. Search one side of the brain, then the other; search through its neurons, dendrites, and axons. Do you find your self in any of those parts? Ask these questions openly, without rushing to an answer.

Feeling

Look for your self in the pleasant, unpleasant, and indifferent feelings you have in response to your senses and thoughts. Do you find your self in these emotional reactions?

Perception
Search for your self in the bundled sensory impulses and thoughts that your mind labels as "objects," "people," and "ideas." Are you this mental factor of perception, that labels and organizes inner and outer reality?

Mental formations
Or do you find yourself in other mental factors like sense contact, attention, or urge—the mental factor that drives you to action?

Consciousness
Now search for your self in the space of your mind—the place where other mental factors appear. Is this space expansive or confined? Bright or dark? Are you the entire space or only some part of it?

The mind can appear as moments of consciousness that grow, abide, diminish, and disappear. Are you any one of those moments? Are you the sum of past moments? Do you find your self only in the present moment, diving forward into each new moment of awareness?

If you don't find your self, let your mind relax into this non-finding. "Self" is merely a label placed on changing mental experience. Realizing this doesn't negate your existence, but simply reveals that the way you exist is much richer, more interdependent, and changing than it ordinarily seems.

DEDICATION
Come back from ultimate reality to conventional reality. Things do exist, but only as labels applied by your mind to collections of parts. Everything comes together through endless chains of causes and effects, including you, who doesn't exist in the solid, unchanging, separate way that makes you feel lonely, needy, and unsatisfied.

The interdependent nature of reality means that you are alive, changing, and interconnected with everything and everyone else in the universe. You can feel and express love and compassion, and your smallest harmful or beneficial acts have lasting impacts on the world and on your mind.

Feel that you have accomplished so much good already today simply by contemplating the heroic arc of these stages of the path. You've increased the strength of beneficial neural pathways to create the causes of a happier, more meaningful and connected life. May all the good from this meditation manifest in helpful, skillful actions and interactions as you go through your day to make the world a more compassionate, just, and joyful place.

The path is empty too

Reaching the end of this book, you may have come to realize that each stage of this Buddhist path isn't sealed off from the next but depends on all the others. As I've meditated on this sequence over the years, there have been many "Aha!" moments when I realized how one part of the path perfectly answers a nagging question that I had about one of its other parts. The path itself is empty, which you now know means that it is interdependent, made of parts, causes, and your mind labeling it as a path to enlightenment.

You may also have noticed how Buddhism appears to be filled with paradoxes, like meditating on suffering being a cause of happiness, or using intellectual thoughts to arrive at non-conceptual realizations. But what each of these seeming contradictions really demonstrates is non-duality: how binary, polarized ways of thinking are not only inaccurate but also harmful to our well-being and to the well-being of our society and environment. That's why Buddhism's "middle way" is so aptly named, encouraging us to find a sustainable, joyful way of living that lies between the extremes of craving and despair, alienation and attachment, apathy and panic.

I sincerely hope that this interdependent psychological toolkit benefits you as much as it has benefited me, so you, too, find that you can cultivate your best qualities and let go of unhelpful habits that get in the way of happiness, human connection, and a meaningful life.

> May all beings have happiness and its causes.
> May all beings be free from suffering and its causes.
> May all beings feel joy that transcends their pain.
> May all beings feel love for those near and distant.

ACKNOWLEDGMENTS

It continues to astonish me that we have access to teachers who maintain Buddhism's unbroken lineage. My own teachers trace their knowledge of these practices back to those who originated them centuries ago in India and Tibet, who in turn trace them back to the Buddha himself. So, I first acknowledge these living masters, beginning with two teachers who have been generous enough to spend thousands of hours with me and other Western students studying and meditating on the lamrim's topics in intricate detail: Geshe Ngawang Dakpa and Venerable René Feusi.

I am also extraordinarily grateful for the hundreds of hours I have spent in larger groups with some of the planet's most highly realized beings, including His Holiness the Dalai Lama, Choden Rinpoche, Ribur Rinpoche, Lama Zopa Rinpoche, and Gyumed Khensur Rinpoche Lobsang Jampa.

I thank the teachers I have spent less time with, but benefited from just as much, including my brother's teacher Geshe Tsulga, Arjia Rinpoche, Venerable Sangye Khadro (Kathleen McDonald), Venerable Robina Courtin, Venerable George Churinoff, the masterful and entertaining scholar Dr Robert Thurman, and the wise and compassionate lay practitioners Elaine Jackson, Rob Preece, Tenzin Chogkyi, Emily Hsu, and Paula Chichester.

For their wisdom, humility, and inspiration, I am beholden to the Buddhist nuns I have worked closely with over the years at Dharma centers, including Venerable Lobsang Chokyi, Venerable Lhundrup Chosang, Venerable Lhundrup Chodron, and Venerable Thubten Drolma (Fabienne Pradelle), former director of the Vajrapani Institute for Wisdom Culture, who has been a supporter of this work since its tentative beginnings.

She gave me the opportunity to develop this program in courses at London's Jamyang Buddhist Centre, where she now serves as the executive director.

I thank my wise and compassionate Dharma friends for inspiration and clarification, including Richard Prinz, Elaine Jackson, Lynne Sonenberg, my *Skeptic's Path to Enlightenment* podcast co-founder Stephen Butler, and out talented producer Tara Anderson.

My editor Lucy Carroll's ebullience for what works (and tactful insights into what doesn't) have helped to make this book clearer and more relevant to its readers, along with my copy editor Michelle Clark's keen eyes. I thank my agent, Michael Mungiello, for his enthusiasm for this project and trust in me as a first-time author, and my book coach, Susan DeFreitas, for patiently teaching me how to capture meaning and delight in prose. This book wouldn't exist without her.

I am indebted to the people who took the time to read and comment on drafts of the manuscript, helping me to see the material through others' eyes and make *How to Train a Happy Mind* far better than it would have been without their feedback: Vicki Mackenzie, Alison Murdoch, Jacob Lindsley, Marco Colnaghi, Abelardo Brenes, Steve Beard, Isabela Acebal, Jason Waterman, sujatha baliga, Venerable Thuben Drolma, Venerable Sangye Khadro, Geshe Ngawang Sonam, and my loving, patient, skeptical wife, Dr Ahna Girshick. I also thank Dr Rick Hanson and Dr Wendy Hassenkamp for reviewing a few scientific claims and references. Despite all the help I have received, of course, all errors and omissions in this work are my own.

Finally, I am thankful to my daughter, Samaya, for joyful interruptions, the delight of witnessing her memorize the lamrim over my shoulder as I revised the manuscript, and her helpful insights into language that might be understandable even to an eleven-year-old.

NOTES

1 Confessions of a Buddhist Skeptic

"Buddhism is not meant to" Interview with Scott Snibbe. 2020. "Geshe Tenzin Namdak on the Mind, Disturbing Emotions, and the Ultimate Nature of Reality." *A Skeptic's Path to Enlightenment* podcast, episode 41, November 4. Available at: www.skepticspath.org/podcast/41-geshe-tenzin-namdak-emptiness (accessed April 2023).

"Don't become a Buddhist" Stephen Batchelor. 1999. "Faith & Reason: No more Buddhists, says Dalai Lama." *The Independent*, May 29.

"The first lamrim" Geshe Sonam Rinchen. 1997. *Atisha's Lamp for the Path to Enlightenment.* Translated and edited by Ruth Sonam. Boston, MA: Snow Lion.

"At the beginning of the fifteenth century, in his Lamrim Chenmo" Tsong-kha-pa. 2014. *The Great Treatise on the Stages of the Path to Enlightenment: Volumes 1–3.* Translated by the Lamrim Chenmo Translation Committee. Boston, MA: Snow Lion.

"During a 2007 talk in San Francisco" His Holiness the XIV Dalai Lama. 2007. *In Praise of Dependent Origination* (2 DVD Set). Hosted by Gyuto Vajrayana Center.

"When I interviewed Buddhist scholar Dr Jan Willis" Interview with Scott Snibbe. 2021. "What Is Enlightenment? With Dr Jan Willis." *A Skeptic's Path to Enlightenment* podcast, episode 90, November 2. Available at: www.skepticspath. org/podcast/what-is-enlightenment-with-dr-jan-willis (accessed April 2023).

"The time has come to find a way" His Holiness the Dalai Lama (Dalai Lama XIV). 2011. *Beyond Religion: Ethics for a Whole World.* San Francisco, CA: HarperOne.

"His Holiness has specifically advised people to practice analytical meditation" Dalai Lama (Dalai Lama XIV). 2019. "Relevance of India's Ancient Tradition in Today's World." Dalai Lama, YouTube, August 5. Available at: www.youtube.com/ watch?v=DPAzMTrNRY0 (accessed April 2023).

"Give up religion, give up Buddhism" Adele Hulse. 2020. *Big Love: The Life and Teachings of Lama Yeshe.* Lincoln, MA: Lama Yeshe Wisdom Archive.

2 What Is Analytical Meditation?

"The recently discovered principle of neuroplasticity" Sharon Begley. 2007. *Train Your Mind, Change Your Brain: How a New Science Reveals Our Extraordinary Potential to Transform Ourselves.* New York: Ballantine Books.

"cognitive behavioral therapy, which uses logic" Leslie Sokol and Marci G. Fox. 2019. *The Comprehensive Clinician's Guide to Cognitive Behavioral Therapy.* Eau Claire, WI: PESI Publishing.

"positive psychology" Martin E. P. Seligman. 2004. *Authentic Happiness: Using the New Positive Psychology to Realize Your Potential for Lasting Fulfillment.* New York: Atria Books.

"the better angels of our nature" American President Abraham Lincoln's first Inaugural Address. March 4, 1861. Available at: https://avalon.law.yale.edu/19th_century/lincoln1.asp (accessed April 2023).

"Of course, there is nothing trivial about external sources of happiness" Dr Alan Wallace. 2016. "What Is Happiness?" Study Buddhism, YouTube. Available at: www.youtube.com/watch?v=FBwRTFGdlc0 (accessed April 2023).

"Some scientific studies back up my teachers' warning" Willoughby B. Britton. 2019. "Can Mindfulness Be Too Much of a Good Thing? The Value of a Middle Way." *Current Opinion in Psychology* 28: 159–65.

"clinically proven meditation techniques to treat mental illness" David A. Treleaven. 2018. *Trauma-Sensitive Mindfulness: Practices for Safe and Transformative Healing.* New York: W. W. Norton.

"spiritual bypass" Robert Augustus Masters. 2010. *Spiritual Bypassing: When Spirituality Disconnects Us from What Really Matters.* Berkeley, CA: North Atlantic Books.

"The ways in which the military employs meditation" Matt Richtel. 2019. "The Latest in Military Strategy: Mindfulness." *New York Times,* April 5.

"scientific dialogues they had had with the Dalai Lama" Wendy Hasenkamp. 2019. "Fruits of the Buddhism-Science Dialogue in Contemplative Research." *Current Opinion in Psychology,* August, 28: 126–32.

"meditation improves health, happiness" Daniel Goleman and Richard J. Davidson. 2017. *Altered Traits: Science Reveals How Meditation Changes Your Mind, Brain, and Body.* New York: Avery.

"most of these studies have been conducted on mindfulness meditation" Cortland Dahl, Antoine Lutz, and Richard Davidson. 2015. "Reconstructing and Deconstructing the Self: Cognitive Mechanisms in Meditation Practice." *Trends in Cognitive Sciences,* September, 19(9): 515–23.

"compassion meditation does indeed increase activity in areas of the brain associated with empathy" A. Lutz, J. Brefczynski-Lewis, T. Johnstone, R. J. Davidson 2008.

"Regulation of the Neural Circuitry of Emotion by Compassion Meditation: Effects of Meditative Expertise." *PLoS ONE*, March 26, 3(3): e1897.

"Other studies have shown the ability of compassion meditation" Jennifer Mascaro. 2022. "The Science of Compassion: What We Know—and Don't Know—About Compassion Has Bold Implications for How We Respond to the Needs of Our Time." Insights, Mind & Life Institute, August 24. Available at: www.mindandlife. org/insight/the-science-of-compassion (accessed April 2023).

"The principle of neuroplasticity" Richard J. Davidson and Antoine Lutz. 2008. "Buddha's Brain: Neuroplasticity and Meditation." *IEEE Signal Process Magazine* (Institute of Electrical and Electronics Engineers), January 1, 25(1): 176–4.

"provides a mechanism for" Wendy Hasenkamp. 2022. "Transforming Minds: How Changing the World Begins with Changing Our Minds." Insights, Mind & Life Institute, August 31. Available at: www.mindandlife.org/insight/transforming-minds (accessed April 2023).

"Neurons that fire together, wire together" D. O. Hebb. 1949. *The Organization of Behavior: A Neuropsychological Theory*. New York: John Wiley & Sons Inc.

"the best measure of success in meditation" Thubten Norbu Ling. 2021. "Lam Rim: Study, Reflect, Meditate with Ven. Sangye Khadro (Session 1)." The Buddhist Center Thubten Norbu Ling, YouTube video course. Available at: www.youtube. com/watch?v=ZXNOBUeKTg0 (accessed April 2023).

3 How to Practice Analytical Meditation

"Smiling releases neuropeptides" Ronald Riggio, PhD. 2012. "There's Magic in Your Smile: How Smiling Affects your Brain." *Psychology Today*, June 25.

"Whether standing, walking, sitting, or lying down" Access to Insight. 2013. *Karaniya Metta Sutta: Good Will.* Translated from the Pali by Thanissaro Bhikkhu. Available at www.accesstoinsight.org/tipitaka/kn/snp/snp.1.08.than.html (accessed April 2023).

"Neurologically, it's supposed to take about two months to establish a new habit" Phillippa Lally, Cornelia H. M. van Jaarsveld, Henry W. W. Potts, and Jane Wardle. 2009. "How are Habits Formed: Modelling Habit Formation in the Real World." *European Journal of Social Psychology*, July 16, 40(6): 998–1009.

4 What Is the Mind?

"five mental factors" In Sanskrit, these five universal mental factors, which are said to occur simultaneously with every moment of consciousness, are sparśa, saṃjñā, vedanā, manasikāra, and cetanā, translated as contact, perception, feeling, attention, and volition. I use Alexander Berzin's less common translation of "urge" instead of "volition" for "cetanā" because its meaning feels more immediately

understandable than "volition" or "intention." See "Mental Urge." Available at Study Buddhism by Berzin Archives: https://studybuddhism.com/en/glossary/mental-urge (accessed April 2023).

"how to use them in everyday life" Ben Connelly. 2016. *Inside Vasubandhu's Yogacara: A Practitioner's Guide.* Somerville, MA: Wisdom Publications.

"a 'controlled hallucination,' as neuroscientist Anil Seth describes it" Anil Seth. 2021. *Being You: A New Science of Consciousness.* New York: Dutton.

"biased toward cooperation rather than selfishness" Dacher Keltner. 2009. *Born to Be Good: The Science of a Meaningful Life.* New York: W. W. Norton & Company.

"Some evidence comes from studies" Matthieu Ricard. 2016. *Altruism: The Power of Compassion to Change Yourself and the World.* New York: Back Bay Books.

"analyzing our bad behavior" Robert M. Sapolsky. 1994. *Why Zebras Don't Get Ulcers.* New York: Henry Holt and Company.

"some scientists take a position between these two extremes" Anil Seth. 2021. *Being You: A New Science of Consciousness.* New York: Dutton.

"the laws of physics are not themselves physical objects" David Deutsch. 2011. *The Beginning of Infinity: Explanations that Transform the World.* New York: Viking.

5 Stage 1: The Precious Life

"Every morning when we wake up, we have twenty-four brand new hours to live" Thich Nhat Hanh. 1991. *Peace Is Every Step: The Path of Mindfulness in Everyday Life.* New York: Bantam Dell.

"Whenever I see someone, I always smile" His Holiness the Dalai Lama with Richard Layard. 2015. "Creating a Happier World: An Afternoon with the Dalai Lama and Friends," filmed in London, September 21. "Dalai Lama in Conversation with Richard Layard." Action for Happiness, YouTube. Available at: www.youtube.com/watch?v=q0HkBfCnPUc (accessed April 2023).

"Why is there something rather than nothing?" Gottfried Wilhelm Leibniz. 1890. "The Principles of Nature and Grace, 1714." In *The Philosophical Works of Leibniz,* translated and with notes by George Martin Duncan, Article XXXII. New Haven, CT: Tuttle Morehouse & Taylor.

"The idea that nothing is something is simply irrational" Interview with Scott Snibbe. 2021. "Ten Questions for Dr Robert Thurman (Part 1)." *A Skeptic's Path to Enlightenment* podcast, episode 41, November 4. Available at: www.skepticspath.org/podcast/10-questions-for-robert-thurman-part-1 (accessed April 2023).

"Cosmos introduced the 'cosmic calendar'" See the updated *Cosmos,* hosted by Neil deGrass Tyson. 2014. "Standing Up in the Milky Way." *Cosmos,* Season 1, Episode 1, March 9. FOX TV.

"In studies of people who practice gratitude regularly" Summer Allen. 2018. "The Science of Gratitude: A White Paper Prepared for the John Templeton Foundation." Berkeley, CA: Greater Good Science Center at University of California, Berkeley. Available at: https://ggsc.berkeley.edu/images/uploads/GGSC-JTF_White_Paper-Gratitude-FINAL.pdf (accessed April 2023).

"This instinctual part of yourself" Robert M. Sapolsky. 1994. *Why Zebras Don't Get Ulcers*. New York: Henry Holt and Company.

"a world that is safer and more abundant for humans" Stephen Pinker. 2011. *The Better Angels of Our Nature: Why Violence Has Declined*. New York: Viking.

6 Stage 2: Embracing Impermanence

"the average civilization lasts only about 350 years" Luke Kemp. 2019. "The Lifespans of Ancient Civilizations." BBC Future, February 20. Available at: www.bbc.com/future/article/20190218-the-lifespans-of-ancient-civilisations-compared (accessed April 2023).

"Millions of your body's cells die every second" Mark Fischetti and Jen Christiansen. 2021. "Our Bodies Replace Billions of Cells Every Day." *Scientific American*, April 1.

"Over the course of a single year, 98 percent of all the atoms in your body are exchanged" David Kestenbaum. 2007. "Atomic Tune-Up: How the Body Rejuvenates Itself." *All Things Considered*, NPR. July 14.

"the hero's journey" Joseph Campbell. 1949. *The Hero with a Thousand Faces*. New York: Pantheon Books.

7 Stage 3: Mental Cause and Effect

"Today, most physicists believe that randomness, not determinism, is at the root of the universe" Joshua Moritz. 2022. "The Ineffable Purpose of Randomness." John Templeton Foundation. Available at: www.templeton.org/news/the-ineffable-purpose-of-randomness (accessed April 2023).

"His Holiness the Dalai Lama makes some clarifying statements" Bhiksu Tenzin Gyatso (Dalai Lama XIV) and Bhiksunī Thubten Chödron. 2019. *Samsara, Nirvana, and Buddha Nature: Volume 3*, The Library of Wisdom and Compassion. Somerville, MA: Wisdom Publications.

"The role of ethics in human behavior" Matthieu Ricard. 2016. *Altruism: The Power of Compassion to Change Yourself and the World*. New York: Back Bay Books.

"Robert Thurman puts this poetically" Robert Thurman. 2021. *Wisdom Is Bliss: Four Friendly Fun Facts that Can Change Your Life*. Carlsbad, CA, and New York: Hay House.

"There is no such thing as an overreaction" Bessel van der Kolk. 2022. Advanced Master Program on the Treatment of Trauma (video course). The National Institute for the Clinical Application of Behavioral Medicine, Storrs, CT.

8 Stage 4: What Do You Do When You Are Alone?

"When I interviewed Dzigar Kongtrul Rinpoche" Interview with Scott Snibbe. 2021. "Dzigar Kongtrul Rinpoche on Patience, Compassion, and Art." *A Skeptic's Path to Enlightenment* podcast, episode 54, February 23. Available at: www.skepticspath. org/podcast/54-dzigar-kongtrul-rinpoche (accessed April 2023).

"Golf Digest published a profile on him" Josh Sens. 2002. "Good Karma, Bad Golf." *Golf Digest*, November.

"neuroscientific research shows that addiction to pornography can lead to problems" Donald L. Hilton and Clark Watts. 2011. "Pornography Addiction: A Neuroscience Perspective." *Surgical Neurology International*, February 21, 2: 19.

"causes the pleasure it brings you to grow weaker" K. M. Sheldon and S. Lyubomirsky. 2021. "Revisiting the Sustainable Happiness Model and Pie Chart: Can Happiness be Successfully Pursued?" *Journal of Positive Psychology*, 16(2): 145–54.

"happiness comes from 'a home inside'" Thich Nhat Hanh. 2014. *How to Love.* Berkeley, CA: Parallax Press.

"Most people live in harmony" Stephen Pinker. 2011. *The Better Angels of Our Nature: Why Violence Has Declined.* New York: Viking.

9 Stage 5: Am I More Important than Everyone Else in the Universe?

"a five-star hotel is a perfect place to meditate" Lama Zopa Rinpoche, translations and instructions. 2011. *The Preliminary Practice of Prostrations to the Thirty-Five Confession Buddhas.* Portland, OR: Foundation for the Preservation of the Mahayana Tradition.

"If things were brought into being by choice" Acharya Shantideva. 1979. "Patience," in *A Guide to the Bodhisattva's Way of Life.* Translated by Stephen Batchelor. Stanza 34, p. 58. Dharamsala, India: Library of Tibetan Works and Archives.

"Robert Thurman prefers to call these the four facts" Robert Thurman. 2021. *Wisdom Is Bliss: Four Friendly Fun Facts that Can Change Your Life.* Carlsbad, CA, and New York: Hay House.

"Just as a seed cannot sprout" Geshe Acharya Thubten Loden. 1996. *Meditations on the Path to Enlightenment.* Yuroke, Victoria, Australia: Tushita Publications.

"Imagine that a person strikes you with a stick" Acharya Shantideva. 1979. "Patience," in *A Guide to the Bodhisattva's Way of Life*. Translated by Stephen Batchelor. Stanza 41, p. 59. Dharamsala, India: Library of Tibetan Works and Archives.

10 Stage 6: The Red Pill of Renunciation

"In the movie's most famous sequence, Morpheus tells Neo that everything about the world he lives in is a lie" *The Matrix*. Warner Brothers Pictures, 1999.

"we are willing to sacrifice something" Dalai Lama XIV and Dr Alexander Berzin. 1997. *The Gelug/Kagyu Tradition of Mahamudra*. Boston, MA: Snow Lion.

"The best way to keep a prisoner from escaping is to make sure he never knows he's in prison" Attributed to Fyodor Dostoevsky but not found in his published works.

"Nobody wants to be anywhere" Jerry Seinfeld. 2021. *23 Hours to Kill*. Netflix.

"fake compassion is narcissism" Interview with Scott Snibbe. 2022. "Buddhist Psychologist Lorne Ladner on Depression, Compassion, and Positive Psychology." *A Skeptic's Path to Enlightenment* podcast, episode 110, June 28. Available at: www.skepticspath.org/podcast/buddhist-psychologist-lorne-ladner (accessed April 2023).

"When we are uncomfortable" *Discovering Buddhism* (DVD), 2004. Portland, OR: Foundation for the Preservation of the Mahayana Tradition.

11 Stage 7: What Is Love?

"we should more precisely call this 'empathy fatigue'" Matthieu Ricard. 2016. *Altruism: The Power of Compassion to Change Yourself and the World*. New York: Back Bay Books.

"the very word for enlightenment, bodhi" Dalai Lama XIV and Thubten Chödron. 2020. *In Praise of Great Compassion: Volume 5*. The Library of Wisdom and Compassion. Somerville, MA: Wisdom Publications.

"utilitarianism" Katarzyna de Lazari-Radek and Peter Singer. 2017. *Utilitarianism: A Very Short Introduction*. Oxford: Oxford University Press.

"stoicism" Massimo Pigliucci. 2017. *How to Be a Stoic: Using Ancient Philosophy to Live a Modern Life*. New York: Basic Books.

"If you would like to be selfish" His Holiness the Dalai Lama (Dalai Lama XIV). 1994. *The Way to Freedom: Core Teachings of Tibetan Buddhism*, The Path to Enlightenment. San Francisco, CA: HarperSanFrancisco.

"James Harrison" Matt Stephens. 2018. "'Man with the Golden Arm' Saved Millions of Australian Babies with His Blood." *New York Times*, May 14.

"Zell Kravinsky" Ian Parker. 2004. "The Gift: Zell Kravinsky Gave Away Millions. But Somehow It Wasn't Enough." *New Yorker*, July 25.

"egoism" Denise Cummins. 2016. "This Is What Happens When You Take Ayn Rand Seriously." PBS News Hour, February 16. Available at: www.pbs.org/newshour/economy/column-this-is-what-happens-when-you-take-ayn-rand-seriously (accessed April 2023).

"If you want to be happy, cherish others" Dalai Lama XIV quoted by Lama Zopa Rinpoche. Lama Zopa Rinpoche. 1986. "Cherish Others and Be Happy." Archive #398. Nepal: Kopan Monastery. Available at: www.lamayeshe.com/article/cherish-others-and-be-happy (accessed April 2023).

"anger is motivating, but it's like taking a powerful drug" His Holiness the Dalai Lama (Dalai Lama XIV). *Be Angry*. Charlottesville, VA: Hampton Roads Publishing.

"a period of anger is often necessary" Tara Brach. 2020. "Sheltering in Love – Part 7: Awakening from the Prison of Blame." Tara Brach podcast, May 6. Available at: www.tarabrach.com/sheltering-in-love-part-7 (accessed April 2023).

"Black civil rights activist Ann Atwater and C. P. Ellis" Michele Norris and Melissa Block. 2005. "Civil-Rights Activist, Ex-Klansman C. P. Ellis," obituary. *All Things Considered*, NPR, November 8. Osha Gray Davidson. 2007. *The Best of Enemies: Race and Redemption in the New South*. Chapel Hill, NC: University of North Carolina Press.

"we remain stuck in some kind of prehistory, unworthy of humanity's great spirit." Kim Stanley Robinson. 2002. *The Years of Rice and Salt*. New York: Bantam Dell, p. 471.

"For as long as space remains" Acharya Shantideva. 1979. "Dedication," in *A Guide to the Bodhisattva's Way of Life*. Translated by Stephen Batchelor. Stanza 55, p. 167. Dharamsala, India: Library of Tibetan Works and Archives.

12 Stage 8, Part 1: How Things Exist

"the 1968 François Truffaut film" François Truffaut. 1968. *Stolen Kisses* (French: *Baisers volés*). United Artists.

"When we try to pick out anything by itself" Stephen Fox. 1981. *John Muir and His Legacy: The American Conservation Movement*. Boston, MA: Little, Brown and Company.

"Emptiness should be understood in the context of dependent arising" His Holiness the Dalai Lama (Dalai Lama XIV). 1999. *The Path to Tranquility: Daily Wisdom*. Edited by Renuka Singh. New York, NY. Penguin Publishing Group.

"a phone contains almost every type of matter in the universe" Magdalena Petrova. 2018. "We Traced What It Takes to Make an iPhone, From Its Initial Design to the Components and Raw Materials Needed to Make It a Reality." CNBC, December 14. Available at: www.cnbc.com/2018/12/13/inside-apple-iphone-where-parts-and-materials-come-from.html (accessed April 2023).

"I think that tastes, odors, colors, and so on" Galileo Galilei, "The Assayer." In S. Drake 1996 [1623]. *The Discoveries and Opinions of Galileo.* New York: Doubleday.

"the Dalai Lama himself says" The nature of reality—theory of relativity, quantum science and Buddhist thought. His Holiness the 14th Dalai Lama of Tibet. 2013. "Mind and Life XXVI: Mind, Brain, and Matter—Critical Conversations Between Buddhist Thought and Science." Drepung Monastery, Mundgod, Karnataka, India, January 17–22.

"I first heard the logic for this from the Dalai Lama" His Holiness the XIV Dalai Lama. 2007. *In Praise of Dependent Origination* (2 DVD Set). Hosted by Gyuto Vajrayana Center.

"For whom emptiness is possible, everything is possible" Nagarjuna's *Mulamadhyamakakarika,* translated by Stephen Batchelor. See Stephen Batchelor. 2000. *Verses from the Center: A Buddhist Vision of the Sublime.* New York: Riverhead Books.

13 Stage 8, Part 2: Who Am I?

"could one day be uploaded to a digital brain" David J. Chalmers. 2014. "Mind Uploading: A Philosophical Analysis." In D. Broderick and R. Blackford (editors). *Intelligence Unbound: The Future of Uploaded and Machine Minds.* Malden, MA: Wiley Blackwell.

"A human being is a part of the whole" Albert Einstein's letter to Alice Calaprice, February 12, 1950. Albert Einstein Archives, Hebrew University of Jerusalem, Israel.

"three ways that people can view their 'I,' or self" Dalai Lama XIV and Dr Alexander Berzin. 1997. *The Gelug/Kagyu Tradition of Mahamudra.* Boston, MA: Snow Lion. Part IV, Session Eight: The Three Ways of Apprehending "Me"

"when people reflect on their sense of self, the brain activates" Anil Seth. 2021. *Being You: A New Science of Consciousness.* New York: Dutton.

"You are only made of non-you elements" Thich Nhat Hanh. 2000. *Going Home: Jesus and Buddha as Brothers.* New York: Riverhead Books.

14 A Skeptic's Path to Enlightenment

"Seeing is forgetting the name of the thing one sees" Lawrence Weschler. 1982. *Seeing Is Forgetting the Name of the Thing One Sees: A Life of Contemporary Artist Robert Irwin.* Oakland, CA: University of California Press.

"May all beings have happiness and its causes" Translation by the author, based on "The Four Immeasurables." In Lama Zopa Rinpoche (translator). *Lama Tsong Khapa Guru Yoga.* Portland, OR: Foundation for the Preservation of the Mahayana Tradition.

FURTHER READING

Secular Buddhism

Stephen Batchelor. 1998. *Buddhism without Beliefs: A Contemporary Guide to Awakening.* New York: Riverhead Books.

Stephen Batchelor. 2015. *After Buddhism: Rethinking the Dharma for a Secular Age.* Newhaven, CT: Yale University Press.

His Holiness the Dalai Lama (Dalai Lama XIV). 1999. *Ethics for the New Millennium.* New York: Riverhead Books.

His Holiness the Dalai Lama (Dalai Lama XIV). 2011. *Beyond Religion: Ethics for a Whole World.* San Francisco, CA: HarperOne.

Robert Wright. 2017. *Why Buddhism Is True: The Science and Philosophy of Meditation and Enlightenment.* New York: Simon & Schuster.

Science, Buddhism, and the mind

Daniel Goleman and Richard J. Davidson. 2017. *Altered Traits: Science Reveals How Meditation Changes Your Mind, Brain, and Body.* New York: Avery.

Rick Hanson, PhD. 2009. *Buddha's Brain: The Practical Neuroscience of Happiness, Love, and Wisdom.* Oakland, CA: New Harbinger Publications.

Rick Hanson, PhD. 2020. *Neurodharma: New Science, Ancient Wisdom, and Seven Practices of the Highest Happiness.* New York: Harmony Books.

His Holiness the Dalai Lama (Dalai Lama XIV). 2006. *The Universe in a Single Atom: The Convergence of Science and Spirituality.* New York: Harmony Books.

Anil Seth. 2021. *Being You: A New Science of Consciousness.* New York: Dutton.

Robert Thurman. 2021. *Wisdom Is Bliss: Four Friendly Fun Facts that Can Change Your Life.* Carlsbad, CA, and New York: Hay House.

Mindfulness and meditation

Thich Nhat Hanh. 1991. *Peace Is Every Step: The Path of Mindfulness in Everyday Life.* New York: Bantam Dell.

Thich Nhat Hanh. 1996. *The Miracle of Mindfulness: A Manual on Meditation.* Boston, MA: Beacon.

Dza Kilung Rinpoche. 2015. *The Relaxed Mind: A Seven-Step Method for Deepening Meditation Practice.* Boulder, CO: Shambala.

The Tibetan Buddhist lamrim

His Holiness the 14th Dalai Lama. 2012. *From Here to Enlightenment: An Introduction to Tsong-kha-pa's Classic Text The Great Treatise of the Stages of the Path to Enlightenment.* Boston, MA: Snow Lion.

Gyumed Khensur Lobsang Jampa. 2013. *The Easy Path: Illuminating the First Panchen Lama's Secret Instructions.* Somerville, MA: Wisdom Publications.

Geshe Acharya Thubten Loden. 1996. *Meditations on the Path to Enlightenment.* Yuroke, Victoria, Australia: Tushita Publications.

Kathleen McDonald. 1984. *How to Meditate: A Practical Guide.* Somerville, MA: Wisdom Publications.

Tsong-kha-pa. 2014. *The Great Treatise on the Stages of the Path to Enlightenment: Volumes 1–3.* Translated by the Lamrim Chenmo Translation Committee. Boston, MA: Snow Lion.

Love and compassion

Tara Brach, *Radical Self-Acceptance* (CD). Louisville, CO: Sounds True, 2008.

Kathleen McDonald. 2010. *Awakening the Kind Heart: How to Meditate on Compassion*. Somerville, MA: Wisdom Publications.

The Dalai Lama (Dalai Lama XIV). 2001. *An Open Heart: Practicing Compassion in Everyday Life*. Boston, MA: Little, Brown and Company.

Thich Nhat Hahn. 2014. *How to Love*. Berkeley, CA: Parallax Press.

Rob Preece. 2009. *The Courage to Feel: Buddhist Practices for Opening to Others*. Boston, MA: Snow Lion.

The nature of reality

His Holiness the Dalai Lama (Dalai Lama XIV) and Jeffrey Hopkins. 2006. *How to See Yourself as You Really Are*. New York: Atria Books.

Khensur Jampa Tegchok. 2012. *Insight Into Emptiness*. Somerville, MA: Wisdom Publications, 2012.

Dalai Lama XIV and Dr Alexander Berzin. 1997. *The Gelug/ Kagyu Tradition of Mahamudra*. Boston, MA: Snow Lion.

Geshe Tashi Tsering. 2009. *Emptiness: The Foundation of Buddhist Thought: Volume 5*. Somerville, MA: Wisdom Publications.

Karma, rebirth, and buddha nature

Dr Alexander Berzin. 2001. "Clearing Away Extraneous Conceptions about Karma." Seminar transcription, Berlin, Germany, March. Available at Study Buddhism by Berzin Archives: https://studybuddhism.com/en/advanced-studies/ lam-rim/karma-advanced/clearing-away-extraneous- conceptions-about-karma (accessed April 2023).

Dr Alexander Berzin and Thubten Chödron. 1999. "Do You Believe in Rebirth?," revised excerpt from *Glimpse of Reality*. Amitabha Buddhist Centre, Singapore, August. Available at Study Buddhism by Berzin Archives: https:// studybuddhism.com/en/tibetan-buddhism/path-to-enlightenment/karma-rebirth/do-you-believe-in-rebirth (accessed April 2023).

Bhiksu Tenzin Gyatso (Dalai Lama XIV) and Bhiksunī Thubten Chödron. 2019. *Samsara, Nirvana, and Buddha Nature: Volume 3*, The Library of Wisdom and Compassion. Somerville, MA: Wisdom Publications.

Dacher Keltner. 2009. *Born to Be Good: The Science of a Meaningful Life*. New York: W. W. Norton & Company, 2009.

Robert M. Sapolsky. 1994. *Why Zebras Don't Get Ulcers*. New York: Henry Holt and Company.

ABOUT THE AUTHOR

Scott Snibbe is a twenty-year student of Tibetan Buddhism whose teachers include Lama Zopa Rinpoche and His Holiness the Dalai Lama. He is the Executive Director of A Skeptic's Path to Enlightenment, a nonprofit organization dedicated to teaching secular forms of Tibetan Buddhist analytical meditation through its podcast, website and courses. Find out more at www.skepticspath.org.